# How to Write
# How-To Books
# and
# Articles

# HOW TO WRITE "HOW-TO" BOOKS & ARTICLES

## RAYMOND HULL

Writer's
Digest
Books

Cincinnati, Ohio

**Library of Congress Cataloging in Publication Data**

Hull, Raymond, 1919-
    How to write how-to books and articles.

    Bibliography: p. 199
    Includes index.
    1. Authorship. I. Title.
PN145.H78          808'.02          81-11653
ISBN 0-89879-057-3          AACR2

Book design by Barron Krody.

# Contents

titles and headings. Accuracy: your contract with the reader. Be concise—but not *too* concise. The benefits of suspense and variety. Avoid the impersonal style—reveal yourself in your writing.

# Introduction

This book tells how you can make money and earn prestige by selling expert knowledge to people who want it via magazines, newspapers, and books.

Do you already have some practice in writing for publication? Are you also an expert in some subject or subjects—guitar playing, gold panning, conjuring, wood carving, tulip growing? Have you discovered or invented something? Do you want to pass on your expertise? Then this book tells you how to break into the field of how-to writing.

Or maybe you are a competent writer, but possess no particular expertise in other subjects. Then you can find nonwriters who have some specialized knowledge, and collaborate with them to put that knowledge into publishable form.

Or perhaps you are an expert in some subject, but have never, up to now, thought of putting your knowledge on paper and selling it for publication. This book will show you how you could do that.

Or maybe you don't care to write yourself, but have thought about collaborating with an experienced writer. To improve your chances of success, you should know how to find a capable collaborator; you should know at least *something* about the writing and publishing business; you should thoroughly understand what your writer-collaborator is doing, and why. This book gives you the information you need. So read it all through. (And bear in mind the possibility that, after some productive collaboration, you might go on to become a successful writer yourself! I've seen it happen.)

I'm looking at a recent annual almanac. Of the year's twenty-four bestselling hardcover nonfiction books, six are on how-to subjects! How-to books are the backbone of every book publisher's "backlist" of consistently selling titles.

Of the 125 big-circulation (over 400,000) magazines listed there, at least one hundred use how-to articles; many of them are entirely how-to!

For years past, every newspaper I've seen contained how-to material!

It's a wide-open territory. Why not stake your claim? There's a thrill in knowing that your technical knowledge and writing are helping other people, that your name is being acknowledged as that of an expert. Think of names such as Dale Carnegie, Napoleon Hill, Arnold Bennett, Roget, Horace, Epictetus, La Rouchefoucauld, Lord Chesterfield, Webster, Mrs. Beeton—famous, wholly or partly, for their how-to writings.

There's a keen personal satisfaction in knowing that you are part of the nonstop process by which our species transmits and perpetuates its skill and knowledge.

One last suggestion. Whatever may be your particular interest in this subject—as nonwriter, beginning writer, or experienced writer—don't stop short at *reading* the book. It contains exercises that lead toward practical, effective understanding and application of the rules and principles offered in the text.

So, whatever parts of the book you mean to apply, *do the relevant exercises*. That way you'll get the full value for your time, mental effort, and money.

# 1

# How-to Writing: An Inexhaustible Field

 It's sometimes called "how-to-do-it" writing; but since I need the phrase several hundred times in this book, I'm using the shorter form, "how-to." (That exemplifies one rule for how-to writing: Waste no space, but explain any abbreviations.)

## Enormous Scope

The how-to category offers enough scope to keep a writer working through ten lifetimes. For many people the phrase "how-to" conjures up thoughts of craft and hobby magazines. True, those magazines are important in the how-to market, but they are only a part of it!

I have before me a special advertising feature section from my morning newspaper. It is all about homes and home living. Sixty percent of the space is taken up with ads; most of the remainder consists of how-to articles:

Fire precautions in your kitchen
The use of photographs in decorating
Do's and don't's for painting inside and outside the home
Beautifying closets
Remodeling kitchens
Insulation to reduce heating costs
Twelve basic tools for do-it-yourself novices

Comfortable living in one room
Decorative treatments for windows with no views
Remodeling bathrooms
Saving electric energy with small appliances
Stimulating decor for children's rooms
Tips for growing healthy indoor plants
Curing squeaky doors
New uses for household trash
Precautions against burglary
Pots and pans in kitchen decor

The Saturday magazine section of my afternoon paper usually carries some how-to articles. This week I see one telling how to start and operate an investment club.

Today my weekly neighborhood newspaper carries a piece entitled "Your Rent: You Must Pay Up," the third in a series of six how-to articles for landlords and tenants, telling what each must and must not do under local legislation. A huge readership here! It includes not only owners of, and renters in, big apartment blocks, it covers every home owner who rents a basement or attic room, and every tenant who sleeps in such a room.

All this is just the beginning. What about how-to books?

I have on my desk a local newspaper containing reviews of recent publications. Here is a half-page review of a 500-page book telling liberated, present-day parents how to raise their children. Some of the parents' goals, says the author, should be to free children from sex stereotyping, to help them do well in school, and to monitor what they watch on television.

Here is a quarter-page review of a book telling men how to look after their clothes: drying wet clothes, removing ink and perspiration stains from shirts, removing wrinkles from neckties, and so on.

Another review covers a big book of simple magic tricks that require no special apparatus, but use objects from the kitchen and living room—string, playing cards, cups, tumblers, and such stuff.

I checked the book division of a department store the other day. They had approximately 1,150 how-to titles on their shelves—close to one-third of the total display space!

Take a look yourself around a library or bookstore. In the single area of sports and games you'll find books on dozens of subjects—archery, boxing, wrestling, judo, ice skating, roller skating (suddenly revived from near-oblivion in the late 1970s), running (think of the books on jogging!), swimming, diving, golf, fishing, badminton, table tennis, squash, weight lifting.

Think of the literature of various religions; much of it tells readers how to live—how to eat, drink, cook, pray, marry, divorce, work, play, speak, trade, and dress; how to summon up spirits, how to exorcise ghosts, and so on.

Many school texts are how-to. There's another insatiable market for anyone who knows how to write for it.

And the demand for books never ceases. Old books grow outdated as new equipment is invented, as rules are modified, as social customs change. (I remember when weight lifting and wrestling were for men, badminton for women.) New experts arise and old records fall. People find better ways to move their arms and legs, to handle their equipment, and to outwit their opponents; sooner or later their techniques become raw material for new how-to books.

Then, too, good old books go out of print, leaving room for new authors to rewrite some of the old material—perhaps in clearer, more interesting ways—for the benefit of present-day readers.

Food and drink; health; home construction, alteration, maintenance, and management; science; theater; movies; television; music; travel; camping; selling and merchandising; business management—such subjects call for a steady stream of new how-to writing. Self-improvement for men and women, old, middle-aged, and young, has been an inexhaustible field from Plato's time up to the present, and will continue so into the foreseeable future.

Obviously, a lot of people are writing and selling how-to articles and books. The demand will continue, why shouldn't you help to meet it?

## The Essentials

Two qualities are essential for good how-to writing: expert knowledge of a subject, and the ability to convey that knowledge effectively on paper.

### Expertise

The authority that goes with successful accomplishment in any subject tends to impress a publisher; without that impression, your writing is not likely to see print. That same authority impresses readers, too; it tends to make them read, clip, and apply a magazine article, tends to make them buy a book for themselves and recommend it, or give it, to their friends.

Are you an expert? Try this test.

1. For how-to writing, theoretical knowledge is not enough. *Practical* expertise is important—the actual skill to carve totem poles, build paper kites, cater banquets, unearth antiquities, or whatever your article or book is about. Can you do, easily and confidently, whatever your subject may require, every time, with no worrying in advance about whether you're going to fail?

Who is the best practitioner you know in your specialty? Count him as 10. Score the absolute beginner as 0. Where do *you* stand on that ten-point scale of practical expertise?

2. Have you achieved public recognition for your knowledge or work—sales, awards, exhibitions, etc? Have you discovered or pioneered anything noteworthy in your field? How long have you been successfully doing whatever it is that you mean to write about? In short, how solid is your reputation?

Many readers—and therefore publishers, who try to think like readers—would tend to trust someone who has a sizable record of accomplishment.

Score yourself from 0 to 10 for the recognition and reputation you have achieved.

3. In some subjects, and in some circumstances, it's possible to go on producing for years, while slipping far out of touch with new ideas, materials and methods, and changes of public taste. Do you know and get feedback from the people who buy, use, or consume your product? Do you find, in reading and talking about your subject, that you encounter any, or many, new factors that you don't understand, or can't accept? Readers and publishers don't want outdated material.

Score yourself from 0 to 10 for being up-to-date in your subject.

4. Have you ever *taught* your subject—to private pupils, through schools, courses, conventions, etc? Do you have at your fingertips, and can you spell accurately, all the names and technical terms connected with your subject? Can you talk fairly fluently about it? How-to writing is, after all, a form of teaching.

Score yourself from 0 to 10 for your ability to communicate about your subject, to teach it.

5. Are you methodical and businesslike in working, letter writing, telephoning, etc? The writer is not indulging in a course of pure self-expression! He is entering upon a series of business transactions, proposing that publishers gamble their money and reputation on him and his abilities. A publisher will, understandably, shrink from someone who shows signs of being a sluggard, a muddler, or a cheat.

Score yourself from 0 to 10 for your business capability.

If you have scored less than 30 points on this test, I suggest that you seriously consider upgrading your expertise in the areas that are weak. Some effort along those lines now will greatly improve your chances of success later, when you begin writing.

**Communicative Skill**

Now, what about that second requirement—the ability to convey expert knowledge effectively on paper? There are certain techniques that will enable you to tell readers what you know, or what your collaborator knows. They are described in detail in the following chapters.

But here, at the outset, I will offer a suggestion: Start small! Don't try to begin your how-to writing career with a book; that is a long, complex project, even when things go smoothly. Get your first experience writing shorter material—articles, book reviews, radio or TV scripts, etc. That is the best way to gain confidence in your ability to turn out words, to order, on your chosen subject.

---

**Exercise 1:1**

Make a little study of how-to authors. Look at the authors' credit notices in magazines (maybe attached to the relevant articles; maybe all together on a separate page). On how-to books, look at the jackets, covers, and inside pages near the front or the back to see the qualifications of their authors.

Do you find these descriptions impressive and convincing, or not?

Try to make your own analysis. What does each author seem to know about his subject? How well has he put it into print? What else has he written?

Score each author, on a scale of 0 to 10, for the impression he makes on you.

---

**Exercise 1:2**

Draft a description of your own qualifications as an author of how-to articles and/or books.

Or if you are a nonwriter who is going to be seeking a writer-collaborator, describe the qualifications of the writer you would like to work with.

---

## Summary

How-to writing: an inexhaustible field.
The qualifications:
   Up-to-date knowledge of the subject.
   Communicative skill.
Careful study of published material helps you write well.

# 2

# Writers and Publishers

Many a writer taps away in his lonely room for years, and never sees the publisher or publishers that he is working for. That is a special difficulty we face in this trade. Photographers, dressmakers, architects, actors, singers, dancers, cooks—such people have close, regular contact with, and receive direct stimulation from, their customers and employers.

We tend to be out of touch with ours; and that disconnection makes our work more difficult and less effective than it need be. The better we understand our publishers, the better we shall be able to get on with them.

What is a publisher? In a small, regional firm, a publisher may be one man running his own business with a secretary, an editor, and a part-time bookkeeper, putting out one small magazine a month, or maybe four or five books a year.

Big national publishers are corporations or multiple partnerships, with scores or hundreds of employees. A major periodicals publisher may put out several more or less related weekly or monthly magazines; in the book field, a big publisher may issue dozens, scores, or hundreds of books a year.

Publishing, in the modern sense of the word, began in Europe with the application, somewhere around 1450, of the art of printing by movable type. (That process had been developed in China several centuries earlier.)

Most early publishing was done by printers; they bought (or stole) poems, stories, plays, and books from writers, and printed and bound them. Some of these printer-publishers opened stores and retailed their books to the tiny minority of the population who could read.

The first printing-publishing business in the North American English colonies was that of Stephen Day, in Cambridge, Massachusetts (1639).

From the writer's point of view, three major technical developments—each in turn—have revolutionized the writer-publisher relationship.

**Power**

When James Fenimore Cooper began writing in the early nineteenth century, the best hand-powered printing presses produced about five sheets a minute. Most freight, including printed matter, was transported by horse-drawn wagon or sailing ship. So magazines and books were few and expensive, and writing was a genteel hobby, pursued mainly by schoolteachers, clergymen, and the like.

As the century rolled on, steam power was applied to paper making, printing, bookbinding, and transportation. Magazines and books became cheap and plentiful. Writers could expect to make money—some, perhaps, even to make a living—from their work. By Charles Dickens's day, the publishing industry was much as it is today.

Modern developments in electronic storage and transmission of words and pictures may soon revolutionize the publishing system we now know; we'll just have to wait and see what differences that revolution will make to writers.

**The Typewriter**

Until the late nineteenth century, authors wrote their material by hand, using quills or steel-nib pens dipped into bottles of ink. The finished product was, obviously, called a manuscript. Mark Twain was already internationally famous before the first practicable typewriter came on the market in 1874.

The publishing industry responded enthusiastically to the new invention. Editors found typescript easier to read than handwriting; authors found that, with practice, they could type several times faster than they could write. There are still a few writers who have not accepted the need to type their manuscripts. They persist in submitting handwritten scripts, which most publishers simply send back, unread.

In recent years, typewriters have been much improved by electric power, correcting ribbons, video display, automatic centering, etc.

But the general method of sending out one's work on a batch of type-written sheets is not likely to change soon.

### The Photocopier

No author should ever send out to a publisher, or lend to a friend, his only copy of a script. The friend's house might burn down, or the script might get lost in the mail. You must make copies of all fin-ished scripts, and of all letters to publishers.

In pen-and-ink days, writers made copies simply by handwriting the material twice over, or by using special copying ink and a screw-powered copying press.

Next came carbon paper to be used with the typewriter; it would yield two or three serviceable copies on thin "second sheets." But a carbon copy looks noticeably different from an original, and a writer's submission to a publisher had to be that original copy. A carbon copy submission was definitely unacceptable! That rule ef-fectively ensured that a writer would approach only one publisher at a time. Any attempt to submit to two or more publishers at once was considered to be unprincipled—much like a man proposing mar-riage to several women at once!

Present-day photocopying processes, at their best, will give sharp black-and-white copies as good as the originals. And note that, un-like carbon copying, photocopying will give you an unlimited num-ber of copies, all of equal quality.

## Playing by the Rules

In order to make a good first impression at the publisher's office, an author's typescript should conform to the rules.

**Typeface.** *Pica* (pronounced pike-uh) is preferred; that prints ten characters to the inch. You can get away with *elite* (twelve charac-ters to the inch), but certainly no fancy typefaces—italic, script, etc. Just the square, print-style letters known as roman type are permissi-ble.

**Ribbons.** Use only black ribbons; editors don't like reds, greens, or violets. Keep the type clean, and change ribbons often enough to give crisp, black impressions; editors and printers dislike peering at blurred, pale gray text.

**Paper.** Only one size of paper is permissible: 8½x11 inches (22x28 cm); anything bigger or smaller is strictly taboo! For the originals of proposals, letters, and scripts, use plain white, and type only on one side of each sheet.

A 500-sheet box is a convenient size for the writer to buy; and from

14- to 20-pound bond is about the right range of thickness. (You don't actually buy your paper by the pound. Those weight numbers are traditional manufacturers' terms, understood by merchants who sell the product—something like dress sizes or shotgun gauges. The higher the bond number, the thicker and more costly the paper.)

Don't use the special paper from which typescript can be erased as easily as pencil marks. That's difficult for editors to write on. And don't use thin onionskin paper; true, it would reduce your postage in mailing scripts, but it would not stand the hard usage that scripts undergo at editorial offices.

**Spacing.** Article and book scripts must be double-spaced: i.e., with one vacant line following each line of type. Leave margins of about 1½ inches (35 mm) at the top, bottom, and both sides. To start each paragraph, indent five spaces.

This layout gives an editor room for writing in corrections, alterations, and printer's directions. It also gives you a fairly close count of the words you use: with pica type, you average 250 words per page; with elite, about 300 words per page.

Don't try to vary this format! I knew one man who for years sent out article scripts that were only one-and-one-half-spaced instead of double-spaced, with ¾-inch margins instead of 1½-inch. He was saving paper and postage, and he thought that editors would not notice the difference. But they do notice! His submissions were regularly rejected. The unconventional format may not have been the *sole* cause of the man's failure; but I unhesitatingly say it *reduced his chances of success.*

Always remember that, at the editorial office, you—by way of your script—*are competing with other writers.* You are one entrant in a big contest or race. The editor's duty is to decide who wins the prize. So give yourself every chance: play by the rules!

**Corrections.** Rough drafts that you work on at home may include lots of overtypings, crossings-out, and written insertions—that's part of the process of revision. But on a final copy, carefully use correction fluid, tape, or ribbon, so that the script looks clean and accurate.

**Separate sheets.** Don't attempt to bind the script in any way; leave the pages loose. A book script can conveniently be mailed in the box the paper came in, with an identifying label glued on the lid.

---

**Exercise 2:1**

Make a shopping list of the supplies you will need for your writing, e.g.:

Paper: 500 white top sheets
      1,000 thin yellow newsprint second sheets
Carbon paper: about 50 sheets
Typewriter and black ribbons
Correction material: fluid, tape, or ribbon
Buy at least some of the materials *now*. This purchase is an important symbol of your determination to write; it gives you a powerful motive to persevere with the work.

---

## Summary

Continually study the publishing business.

Always use the typewriter and proper script layout.

Check publishers' preferences on photocopying and simultaneous submissions.

# 3

# Articles and Other Short Pieces

 I mentioned in Chapter 1 the tactical value of beginning with *small* projects. I emphasize "small" because, even though you think you are beginning modestly, you may fail if you attempt *too much, too fast*.

Many a would-be writer, full of enthusiasm, starts off on the wrong foot; he hammers out, in three or four pages, a highly condensed version of all he knows and thinks about his special subject, and mails it to some magazine he would like to have his name in. Usually the script comes right back.

After half a dozen such rejections, he begins to suspect that there is some kind of clique getting all the writing assignments. He thinks he can never penetrate that inner circle. His interest in writing evaporates; he throws away his notes and script; he abandons all hope of becoming a writer.

Yet in reality there is no clique; new people are constantly breaking into the writing business. There are ways to improve your chances of success. Read on!

## Study the Market

The typical purchaser of a magazine or newspaper reads, more or less intently, the items that interest him, and ignores the rest. He never thinks what a complex, wonderful product this is. But, for the writer, that casual attitude won't do!

The would-be maker of shoes, or automobiles, or motion pictures carefully studies the tastes and needs of his potential customers. You must do likewise.

Unlike a book, a periodical (magazine or newspaper) appears at regular intervals—daily, weekly, monthly, quarterly. A book comes into print on a certain date, and although it may be partially revised at some unpredictable future time, for some years its text will remain the same. With periodicals, the title remains the same, but the text differs from issue to issue.

Most newspapers, and some magazines, are printed on cheap paper and put together in flimsy fashion; they will not stand much handling before beginning to fall apart. Other magazines, though of the typical magazine shape, use such paper and binding that they will last for years, and can be saved and used for reference.

## New Material

Most of the material printed in periodicals is *new* to the readers, and much of it is of only fleeting interest; by the next day, or the next week, it will be forgotten. Those parts of it that have lasting value may eventually be incorporated into books.

So the successful periodical writer must always be on the lookout for *new* information, *new* ideas, relevant to the subject or subjects that he wants to write about.

Daily newspapers employ full-time, salaried staff—reporters, columnists, editors—to research and write the enormous amounts of new material that they need every day. They also buy material from news services. Those services have their own reporters and editors, but do not themselves publish; they sell material to newspapers, which pay for the right to use it.

Papers also buy material from syndicated columnists. Each syndicated columnist specializes in one subject—some of them write on how-to subjects—and, through an agent, sells his column to as many newspapers as he can.

Some daily newspapers also buy articles, one at a time, from local freelance writers. (The freelancer is self-employed, generally chooses his own subjects, and sells his writing wherever he can. Most freelancers write part-time.) See if your own paper uses freelance articles. Here are a few clues.

(a) Freelance articles are not likely to be mixed in the general "news" parts of the paper: you are more likely to see them near the editorial pages, or in some of the "special interest" sections—arts, books, theater, gardening, fashion, etc.

Watch the bylines—the authors' names on articles. Those that appear regularly—daily, biweekly, or weekly—are probably staff writers or steady outside contributors. But you may see other names occurring just once, or only rarely: those may be freelancers.

Some papers give a one-line description of each freelancer they publish: "So-and-So is a beekeeper from Honeydale"; "Such-and-Such is a retired County Court judge"; "Who-and-Who is a local writer."

(b) Ask around among local writers and librarians.

(c) Phone the paper and ask if they accept freelance articles.

If this market is, in fact, open, and if your subject is not already being thoroughly covered, then you can try to break in.

Weekly newspapers, by reason of their slower publishing cycle, put less emphasis on up-to-the-minute news than the dailies. Also, the weeklies usually cover less territory than the dailies. A big daily may circulate over an entire state, or even farther; a weekly may cover just one town, or one section of a city.

Most weekly newspapers depend less on full-time staff than does the typical daily. Therefore the weekly is a better market for freelance articles and columns. Some of these can very well be on how-to subjects.

Some daily newspapers publish weekly "magazine" sections, different in format and content from their news pages. Many of these weekly magazines are open to freelance contributions. There, too, some how-to subjects may be acceptable.

The slow publishing cycle of a monthly magazine bars it from trying to present what a newspaper reader would call "news." Nevertheless, the editor wants material that is fresh to his readers. Sometimes that will take the form of a more detailed treatment of material that has been lightly or incompletely touched on in the newspapers.

### Advertising

An important aspect of the periodical press is the advertising that it carries. The publisher of a magazine or newspaper knows pretty well how many people read each issue. He finds out, as accurately as he can, what sort of people they are—their age, sex, education, income, politics, hobbies, spending habits, and tastes.

He sells space to advertisers who want to reach some or all of those readers with their commercial messages. The revenue from the advertising pays a large part of the costs of publication. Without advertising, the periodical press, as we know it, could not survive.

Thanks to the revenue from advertising, a metropolitan daily newspaper can sell for fifty cents a Sunday edition that contains as much reading matter as fifty dollars' worth of hardcover books. Thanks to advertising, a slick monthly magazine, the near-equivalent in size, paper, and printing of a good illustrated book, sells for 10 percent of the price.

For the writer seeking to understand the readers of any newspaper or magazine, the golden rule is "Study the advertisements!"

What are the hopes and fears of that group of readers? What are their tastes in food and clothing? What hobbies do they pursue? What are their virtues and vices? What are their levels of education? How much money do they spend on their various interests?

Study the advertisements, and you will find the answers to those questions, and many more.

---

**Exercise 3:1**

Take one newspaper and one monthly magazine. From the advertisements in each, draw a 500-word economic, physical, and psychological profile of a typical reader.

---

## Fillers: A Good Place to Start

Many magazines and newspapers use "fillers." The name derives from one common function of these little pieces: to fill in odd spaces at column ends.

The filler is shorter than normal article length, ranging from 500 words down to 20 words. Usually it does not have the full article structure—opening, body, conclusion—but just gives one fact, anecdote (serious or comic), bit of advice, personal experience, solution to a problem, or what have you.

For example, a handicrafts filler could briefly describe some new material that has just been invented or put on the market: a glue, a paint, a fabric, a solvent, a tool, a gadget. In other fields, a filler might mention a new variety of flower, fruit or vegetable, a new kind of typewriter ribbon, a recipe, the breaking of some record, an instructive quote from some expert, etc., etc.

Here are some hints for writing and selling fillers.

1. Keep yourself up-to-date. Read widely and constantly in your specialty.

2. Get yourself on the mailing lists of manufacturers, wholesalers, clubs, associations, government departments—any organizations that are likely to provide information on your subject.

3. Regularly visit and talk with retailers. They can often tell you about public reaction to present products and services; they are among the first to hear about public demand for new products and services.

4. Mix regularly with other devotees of your subject; from them you will get information, anecdotes, and ideas. Brief reports of local people's achievements, awards, exhibitions, contests, inventions, etc., could make useful items for you.

5. Study the magazines and papers you read. See what kind and

lengths of how-to fillers they use. These will be the kind for you to write.

6. Study writers' directories, where many publications describe their requirements for fillers.

7. Usually, no querying is necessary for fillers. Script format is the same as for an article. Just send in the script with a self-addressed, stamped envelope for return.

Selling fillers can be an excellent start for a how-to writing career.

## Book Reviews

You may find a market in newspapers—daily or weekly—and in magazines, for reviews of how-to books, especially those that have some local interest. Check local publications to see if anyone is supplying this need. Even if they are, there may still be room for you! Many newspapers and magazines are chronically short of *reliable* reviewers.

So, if you see any kind of opportunity for this work, offer your services by letter, along with a sample book review, to some local newspaper or magazine.

If the editor decides to give you a trial, he will, from time to time, send you a book that he wants reviewed. Examine the reviews he already uses for the length and format he prefers, and his policy on illustrations.

You get to keep the books that he sends you, and you also get a modest fee for the reviews that are used. Moreover, the delivery of some good reviews might well lead on to bigger, better-paying assignments—articles or columns.

The major point to consider in judging a how-to book must be: "How well does it teach the subject it is supposed to teach?"

Stylish writing, pretty pictures, beautiful printing—these are in vain if the book fails in its essential *how-to* function.

---

**Exercise 3:2**

Write a 500-word review of some good how-to book that you have recently read.

---

## Writers' Directories

Whether you're writing a filler, a review, or an article, you must ask yourself who might want to buy it.

Writers' directories are annual books that list, among other features, the titles, addresses, and article requirements of magazines. (For the titles of some writers' directories, see "Marketing Information" in the "Recommended Reading" appendix.)

Also, you will often see in a magazine's directory listing a precise description of the style of writing that it wants.

---

**Exercise 3:3**

Find the titles and addresses of three magazines that might be interested in your article.

---

## Asking for Information

Most magazines are forced to waste considerable office space and staff time handling queries and scripts absolutely irrelevant and useless to them. Even with scripts they would like to buy, some require disproportionate amounts of editorial work to make them fit for publication.

In hope of reducing this waste and annoyance, many magazines will send "Writers' Guidelines" on request—leaflets telling just what subject matter they want, and how they want scripts to be prepared. It would be worthwhile to ask for these guidelines before you even draft a query to these magazines.

Some magazines also offer to send free sample copies to would-be writers. That's useful, of course, but I think you would do well to also buy (or consult in your library) several more copies of such magazines.

## Query Letters

Short story writers generally have to write their scripts first, and then try to find publishers. For articles, the write-first-sell-afterwards procedure is usually wrong.

The customary way to begin is with a query, a letter briefly describing the proposed article and your qualifications to write it. Many magazine editors don't even read unsolicited scripts! So, for success in article writing, you must learn to write good queries first.

### The Address

Don't be too easily satisfied with addressing your query letter simply to "The Editor." It's better if you can find out the name of the individual to whom your letter should go.

Check the listing of the magazine in a writers' directory; see if it gives the names of the people in charge of various departments. Also study the magazine itself; you may be able to find the names of the editorial staff. Many magazines name a separate "Articles Editor"; some big ones list individual editors who handle different kinds of articles.

It is courteous, it is taken as a compliment, it is a sign of your businesslike attitude, to address the right person.

## How to Begin

Make it clear, from the first line, that this is not just an ordinary "letter to the editor," but a query. A good, multipurpose beginning is:

"Would you be interested in an article entitled
So And So"
Center your proposed title on the page, and underline it.

Next, type out a few sentences—fifty words or so should be enough—from that strong, attention-getting opening you have planned for the article.

That will show the editor several things:

(a) a sample of your writing style;

(b) how well you understand the needs and interests of his readers;

(c) how directly you can appeal to those interests, to capture the readers' attention.

Spend a lot of time and effort in polishing that opening. If it is sloppy, a busy editor may read no further. (You don't have to eat all of an egg to know that it's bad!) If it is good, he will feel pleased; he will look with interest at the body of the letter.

## The Body

After that opening sample, several important bits of information should form the body of your query.

(a) Define your subject—if it has not already been made clear by your title and opening.

(b) Summarize what you intend to say about the subject; show the main points that you mean to cover; define the theme.

(c) If your subject and material are fresh, say so. (Check back issues of the magazine to be sure someone else has not forestalled you.)

For example, I could not claim that "How to Write Query Letters" is a fresh subject. This is just a fresh treatment of an old subject.

But, at the time I write, "How to Query Editors by Video-Display System" could qualify as a fresh subject. (Though before this book goes out of print, it will be a common procedure.)

(d) If your subject, or the magazine's policy, requires illustrations, say how many and what sort you can supply. Each magazine's listing in writers' directories says what photo format(s) they prefer.

(e) Mention your sources of information, especially if they are exclusive.

(f) Mention your own special qualifications, if any; for example, a long, intimate, practical knowledge of the subject.

List, by title and magazine, *a few* of the articles you have already had published. Choose those that will carry the most weight for this magazine and this subject.

For example, suppose I want to sell a writers' magazine an article called "Tips on Typewriter Maintenance." It will not carry much weight to mention that I once sold an article on "Cultivating the Jerusalem Artichoke" to a gardening magazine. It would be more useful if I could cite sales of articles on other small-scale mechanical maintenance subjects—bicycles, clocks, cash registers, etc.

But, if you have had nothing published so far, *don't* mention *that*.

(g) State the length you propose to write. Most magazines have several standard lengths that they like to use; you can see them specified in writers' directories. From your study of back issues, you know what proportion of the various lengths they use.

For your first contact with a magazine, don't be over-ambitious: don't aim for their maximum length. Suggest one of the intermediate lengths by asking, "Would you like to see x thousand words on this?"

That can very well be the end of your query letter.

## General Hints

Don't make your query too long. One page, single-spaced, in regular business-letter format, should be enough.

Try to make the letter *interesting*. Briefly mention some of the most startling, useful, important facts that you intend to use. The whole letter, not just the opening sample, is demonstrating your ability as a writer to capture and hold the attention of a reader, and to convey information clearly.

Make the letter perfect in spelling, grammar, and typing.

Enclose a stamped, self-addressed envelope for the editor's reply.

Don't bother telling the editor you are a regular reader of his magazine. Your query letter will show well enough whether you are familiar with the magazine and understand what it is trying to do, for whom.

Don't apologize for "trespassing on your patience," "using your valuable time," etc. It is part of an editor's job to read query letters; if yours is a good one, he will not feel that it is an intrusion.

Don't send exhibits—clippings, documents, diagrams, photographs, etc. The letter must succeed or fail on its own merits.

---

## Exercise 3:4

Write and send a query letter for your article.

---

## Simultaneous Submissions

From magazine listings in writers' directories, you can see the various publishers' policies on simultaneous submissions—offering one's work to several publishers at the same time.

(a) Some publishers say that they will consider simultaneous submissions, and will read photocopies of scripts. It is generally understood that, if you do make simultaneous submissions, you should inform each publisher. You do that, in the query letter, simply by adding "This is a simultaneous submission." You do not need to reveal the names of the other magazines you are submitting to.

(b) Some magazines will not consider simultaneous submissions, but will read photocopies of scripts. For them, if you do send a photocopy, you should add a note, "This is not a simultaneous submission."

(c) Some publishers say nothing in their directory listings about photocopies or simultaneous submissions. You may assume that they want exclusive queries and typed submissions.

In any case where you are doubtful about it, don't try multiple querying or sending photocopied scripts. Feelings run high on this subject. One publisher told me, "If ever I caught a writer making a simultaneous submission to me, I'd never have any dealings with him again."

(N.B. Some publishers' directory listings refer to "Xeroxed submissions." "Xerox" is the trade name of one multiple-copying machine, and is often used as a generic term for all photocopying methods.)

---

**Exercise 3:5**

While waiting for a reply to your query, draft your article and put it through several rewrites. (N.B. This is not the normal procedure; but it's good practice, and you may as well make use of your waiting time while you are studying article writing.)

---

## The Editor Writes

A correctly written query, with a stamped, self-addressed envelope, will unfailingly get some kind of reply from a magazine editor. How soon? That may be anywhere from a few days to a few months. Many magazines advertise their standard reply times in writers' directories, with such phrases as "Reports in 1-3 weeks," "Reports in 2-4 weeks," etc.

But don't panic if the reply does not come precisely within the specified period. Problems at the editorial office—sickness, vacations, resignations, firings, changes of management, etc.—may disrupt the schedule that they usually keep.

Anyway, when the reply does arrive, it will probably be in one of four forms.

(a) The editor says he does not want to see your article. You need not feel too discouraged by such a rejection. Maybe your proposal was good, but the magazine already had bought an article on the same subject by another writer. (That's quite likely to happen with a timely subject!)

The thing to do is to draw up a new query letter, precisely aimed at some other magazine, and mail it out.

Only when a proposal has been rejected by every magazine in the field should you lay it aside. Even then, keep it in mind; you may come across fresh information about the subject that would justify planning a new article and writing a new query. The more thoroughly you know your subject, the more likely this is to happen.

(b) The editor rejects the present query, but suggests that you should try him again with another subject. This is an encouraging sign. For some reason, he does not want the article you are now offering, yet your letter makes him think you are the kind of writer he would like to deal with.

Good strategy here is to send Query No. 1 elsewhere, as suggested in (a) above. Then, as fast as you can, query this editor on some other appropriate subject. Your prompt acceptance of the invitation to query again will consolidate the good impression you have already made.

(c) The editor says he would like to see the article described in your query. He may suggest a date by which he would like to have it. He will probably say how many illustrations, of what kind and format, he wants.

Don't interpret this reply as a promise to buy the article. But it is an important step along the road to a sale. Your query has served its purpose.

There is no need to reply at this stage, "Thank you for your letter of such-and-such date. I will indeed go ahead and write the article as fast as I can." The editor assumes that, when he gives you the go-ahead, you *will* write the article. Wasting your time and his with a letter like this makes you appear amateurish and unbusinesslike.

Just set to work and write the article, precisely as described in your query. Those last six words are not superfluous! I have heard of writers delivering scripts quite different from their queries—even on different subjects! Such antics, of course, annul any good impression made by your query letter.

If there is a deadline, be sure you meet it. Even if there is no deadline, don't delay too long—not more than a month.

Mail the script in an envelope big enough to hold the sheets flat. If photos are enclosed, put a cardboard stiffener in the envelope and mark on the outside: "Photographs. Please Do Not Bend."

Enclose another self-addressed, stamped envelope to bring the script back if it is rejected. Also enclose a brief note referring to the previous correspondence.

(d) The fourth possible response to your original query is that the editor says he is interested, but does not want the article precisely as you have outlined it. Would you be willing to make certain changes?

He may ask for deletion of one or more items you proposed, and a reduction in total length. He may ask for expansion of the article to a greater length than you proposed. He may want some change of theme.

Normally, you would take such a letter as a first-class opportunity. Send him a short note saying you will do what he asks. Then write your article, incorporating his suggested amendments, as fast as you can.

The editor will be pleased if you do a good job. There are a lot of writers who can turn out useful scripts following their own plans; there are far fewer who can write effectively to order! Editors like to discover such writers, and can often find work for them to do.

---

**Exercise 3:6**

Proceed with your article, re-querying, revising, etc., according to what Editor No. 1 says in his reply.

---

## Special Sales Tactics

1. Don't bother sending queries for very short pieces—750 words or less. There is obviously not much point in composing a 350-word query, and going through the whole correspondence procedure, to let the editor see a 700- or 500-word article. Just write the script and send it in with a stamped, self-addressed envelope. No accompanying letter is needed.

2. Don't try to query for a humorous article. (N.B. Don't overlook the possibilities of good, humorous how-to writing!) Only the complete script can show whether you have the rare, precious ability to be funny in print.

3. You will notice that some magazines, in their directory listings, say that they will look at queries or complete scripts. What to do here?

I suggest that, if you already have a complete script that has been rejected elsewhere, you might as well send that. But don't tell the editor that it has already been rejected by one or more of his competitors! And be sure that the script looks brand-new, with no mark of its previous travels and editorial handlings.

Editors have feelings, you know! They don't like to have it

rammed down their throats that they are being offered other people's castoffs. An editor once said, wistfully, to me, "It would be nice if they'd retype *just the first page.*"

But, if you do not have a complete script, stick with the query-first procedure until you get at least some encouragement from an editor to go ahead.

4. A few magazines say they want complete scripts only—no queries. You will have to follow that rule if you want to submit to them.

5. Many daily newspapers will look at scripts, submitted by writers in their circulation area, without any query procedure. They receive, from would-be writers, a lot of amateurish nonsense; a slick-looking article, beautifully typed, and well-aimed at some substantial group of their readers, will stand out like a rosebush growing on a garbage dump.

There are instances where such a well-written, well-aimed submission has led to work as an occasional or regular columnist.

6. In many weekly newspaper offices there is an informal, folksy atmosphere. There you can, if you like, deliver your script in person, and maybe have a talk with the editor himself. If it's a how-to column that you are proposing—gardening, pet care, cooking, shoppers' guide, etc.—you should take along, not just one, but three sample columns to show the editor that you are not a one-shot writer.

## Article Structure

Every good article needs a theme, a precise definition of the main idea that you are trying to convey to the reader.

Let me illustrate what I mean by "theme." Take the previous section of this chapter, "Advertising." Suppose I were writing an article on that for magazine readers, i.e., nonwriters. The theme could be "Your personality is revealed by the advertisements in the magazines you read."

Aiming at *you, the writer,* my theme was "Study of a magazine's advertising helps you understand its readers."

The two pieces might contain most of the same facts, but the two different themes would produce markedly different treatments of the subject!

---

### Exercise 3:7

Clip out two or three articles on your favorite subject that you have recently read and enjoyed. (For convenient reference, I'll call these the "published sample.") Analyze each one; discover and write out the theme.

---

## Exercise 3:8

For some article you would like to write (I'll call this "your article"), define the theme precisely, briefly. Type it on a slip of paper; lay it out or pin it up where you will see it as you write.

N.B. The theme need not always be written verbatim in the article. But it's necessary that you have it, *for your own guidance,* in writing. Every sentence must be relevant to that theme!

For the writing of the article, use a basic three-part structure:
Opening
Body
Conclusion

## The Opening

For a strong, attention-getting opening, imagine that the reader is asking you these three questions.

"What are you writing about?"

"Why is that subject important *to me?*"

"Why should I read it *now?*"

Answer those questions, directly or indirectly, in the first fifty words, and you have a good opening.

That third question must be considered because, as I said earlier, newspaper and magazine editors generally want some element of novelty, of immediacy, in the material they buy.

Take, for example, a suburban weekly newspaper; it's probably not the place for articles on the history of man's domestication and development of wild food and flowering plants. Its readers want practical advice on what to do *here,* in their own gardens, *this week.*

But suppose plant breeders have just produced some marvelous new rhododendron, or tomato, that is particularly suited to the local soil and climate, and that, for good results, should be bought and planted *right now.* That item has the essential timely touch, and would be good material for a how-to article or column.

## Exercise 3:9

Find out how the author of each published sample article has answered the reader's three opening questions.

## Exercise 3:10

For your article, answer, in one sentence each, the reader's three opening questions.

## The Body

For a coherent, smoothly moving, interest-sustaining body, decide what points you want to cover—not too many! Don't make the common error of trying to tell all you know in one script. For the typical article, four or five points, all relevant to the theme, are usually enough.

Then look for, and vividly describe, the *conflict* in each point. Typical how-to conflicts: search for the right materials; criticism and obstruction from family, government, etc.; financial difficulties; the need for practice, study, experimentation, etc.; natural obstacles—cold, heat, humidity, aridity, etc.; public apathy, etc.

Writing that suggests that any how-to project is one smooth, easy glide to success is insincere, uninteresting, and unhelpful. It is your job to show how the problems are solved and success is attained.

---

## Exercise 3:11

For each published sample article:
   (a) Analyze the main points the author has made.
   (b) Find the conflict in each point.
   (c) How, in each case, is that conflict resolved?

---

## Exercise 3:12

For your article:
   (a) Define the main points you are going to make.
   (b) Specify the conflict in each point.
   (c) Decide what solution to recommend to your readers in each case.

---

## The Conclusion

You should not simply make the last main point of your article and come to a dead stop. That leaves the reader feeling dissatisfied, even annoyed. At the end of a phone call or a face-to-face conversation with a friend, you would normally say a few pleasant words to create a graceful conclusion. Something of the same kind is needed in article writing.

Some good concluding techniques: sum up the main points you have made; state your theme; give the reader some final words of advice; offer some brief suggestion for proceeding further with the subject, or mention some future writing you will be doing on the subject.

The effect should be to leave the reader feeling pleased with the article, and feeling eager to get on with doing whatever you have described.

**Exercise 3:13**

From each published sample article, see what the author has used for a conclusion. Analyze the precise effects it is supposed to produce.
  What does it tell the reader?
  How will it make the reader feel?
  What will it make the reader do?

**Exercise 3:14**

For your article, plan a good conclusion.
  What will it tell the reader?
  How will it make him feel?
  What will it make him do?

## Article Script Format

Use 8½x11-inch (22x28-cm) white paper, 16- to 20-pound bond.

At the top left-hand corner of the first page, type your name and full address. The title of the article goes about one-third down the page, centered and underlined.

The text is typed, double-spaced, with margins of about 1½ inches (35 mm) at the top, bottom, and sides.

For pages after the first, put your surname in the top left-hand corner and the page number in the top right. At the bottom of each page, except the last, put (more)—meaning more pages follow. At the end of the article, put the symbol ###, centered, to indicate it is the last page.

Do not staple or clip the sheets of the script together; do not bind them in any sort of cover.

Send to the magazine the top, white copy of the script (unless you know they look at photocopies); be sure to keep a carbon or photocopy for yourself. You will need this if, as sometimes happens, the editor wants you to make some alterations.

## Purchase Procedures

Most magazines advertise in writers' directories the rates that they offer. Some pay by the word; some pay so much per printed page; some pay flat fees, more or less proportional to the length of the articles.

Most magazines have sliding scales of pay. In some, the top rate is about 20 percent above the base; in others it goes up to 50 or 100 percent above the base.

For your first sale to any magazine, you will probably start at the base rate. If your work is good, and if you keep submitting and selling to the magazine, you may expect to move up the scale.

An editor likes to build a "stable" of steady writers who will keep coming up with good proposals of their own. He likes it even better if some of them can write to order on subjects suggested by the edi-- tor.

Some magazines pay "on acceptance": i.e., the editor sends you a check for the full fee with the letter that says he will buy your script.

Some magazines pay "on publication": i.e., when the issue containing your article goes on sale. With a monthly, that will probably mean a delay of two or three months at least, because editors like to work several issues ahead. If your material has special seasonal reference—sports, gardening, fashion, etc.—the delay may be up to a year.

Writers feel, with some justification, that paying on publication is objectionable. But it's a long-established system, and when you are starting out you must grin and bear it.

### Rights

Now, just what are you selling when a magazine buys your how-to article?

Some magazines buy "all rights." When you have sold all rights, the article belongs completely and permanently to the magazine. You have no further connection with the article except that you will be credited as the writer of it, and it may help to build your reputation.

Some magazines buy "first North American serial rights." That does not mean that the article is going to be published by installments; it is just a legal phrase that means you have sold to that magazine the rights of first publication in this continent. You retain all other rights to the article. You may, if you can, sell it later for reprinting in another periodical (although you must not conceal the fact that it has already been printed once).

You could perhaps use it verbatim as a chapter in a book, or sell it to some other writer to be so used. You may make whatever use of it you like; once the "first rights" magazine has published the article, it is yours again! These other rights can, in some cases, be valuable, so don't simply file away and forget old scripts once they have been published. Review those files from time to time to see if you can find some way to make more money out of the old material.

Note that some of the magazines that buy "all rights" will, after publication of an article, release other rights to you if you make a written request. Don't hesitate to do that if you see any chance of profiting by it!

## General Selling Strategy

I am aware that there is some disagreement among writers as to what is the best article-selling strategy. You will notice it yourself after you have attended several courses and writers' conferences, and read several books on writing.

Some undoubted experts tend to downgrade the query letter, and prefer the sending out of complete scripts.

Some experts emphasize the value of verbal contact, by phone or face to face, with editors.

Some experts strongly urge multiple submissions; others don't use the system at all.

There are, in fact, no universal, cast-iron rules. If you live in or near a city where several magazines are published and if you get to know some editors on a first-name basis, drink with them, party with them, go to bed with them, etc., then there is obviously no need for sending formal queries to them.

I have described what I believe to be good methods of selling articles, for anyone new in the field. As you gain experience, as you get to know more editors, you can develop a selling strategy that suits your particular talents, your range of subjects, and the contacts you make.

But certainly, for starters, it's hard to beat the effect of a *really good* query letter! And, as you become a faster, better writer, you should aim to have several good queries on different article ideas out to different magazines at the same time, all the time.

## Continued Study

Some of the exercises in this chapter have described ways of learning by analyzing a few good articles—the published sample. I certainly don't mean to imply that by analyzing *those* articles you are going to learn all you need to know!

Repeat the process; analyze dozens, scores, hundreds of articles. Form the habit of analysis, so that *every time* you read an article you consciously look for the technical means the author has used.

"Exactly why did he put *that* bit of information *there*?"

"Why did he use *this* word instead of some other?"

"Just what means did he use to capture and *sustain* my interest?"

Moreover, when you come across the occasional bad article (yes, editors do sometimes slip up!), analyze it with particular care to find out precisely *why* it is bad. Try to find what *you* could have done to improve it.

Thus, your *reading*, while continuing as a source of pleasure and information, also becomes a nonstop instruction course in the art of *writing*.

Here's an example of such analysis. My evening paper runs a weekly gardening how-to column, tucked in among the "Houses for Sale" classified ads. The mid-April day that I'm writing this page, that column is about hedge planting.

The title answers the question "What are you writing about?" It says "Hedge Your Investment with a Hedge."

"Why is it important to *me*?" (N.B. That does not refer to me, Raymond Hull, the apartment dweller, but to "me," the browser among real estate ads.) The columnist says that:

(a) Hedges add privacy to garden or patio.

(b) Hedges block unwanted noise from the street, or from neighbors.

(c) Good hedges add to the investment value of a home.

"Why should I read it *now*?" The writer says that bundles of dormant hedging shrubs are available *now*—a good value, and best planted *promptly*, before they come into leaf.

The body of the article goes on to give detailed instructions for planting the shrubs and tending them through the first year's growth.

The conclusion gives a list of seven recommended types of shrubs for quick growth into hedges.

For this subject, and for these readers, it's a first-class example of article-writing technique.

## Summary

Understand the operation and requirements of the periodical press.

A prime feature: constant need for *new* material.

Study advertisements to understand readers.

Try reviewing books about your specialty.

Writers' directories give marketing information.

*Good* query letters help sell articles.

Follow each magazine's policy on photocopying and simultaneous submissions.

Be businesslike in dealing with editors.

Try to profit by editors' advice.

Short pieces, humor, newspapers—no querying.

Before you start the article, define the theme.

Article structure: opening; body; conclusion.

Always use correct article script format.

Check what rights in your material you are selling.

Consider reuse of once-published articles.

Don't just *read* articles; *analyze* them, to improve your own writing.

# 4

# Planning a Book

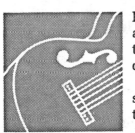 I've emphasized the technical and emotional advantages of starting small: You learn your trade by easy installments; you reduce the risk of severe disappointments.

OK. So you've started small. Now, when should you consider that you are ready to tackle a book?

I began selling magazine articles in 1959. Around 1965 I was living—modestly, to be sure—by my writing, and by teaching writing courses.

My first book was published in 1968. But note: That was my *first* attempt at book writing; it was bought by the *first publisher* who saw the proposal; and, in several editions, in two languages, that book is *still* selling briskly.

This prompt, substantial success with the book came, I think, because I was *thoroughly prepared* by the writing and selling of articles and other short pieces.

I'm not prescribing that you exactly imitate my schedule. I suffered a lot of delays and distractions: much of the writing I did from '59 to '68 was for radio, TV, and the stage—not nonfiction at all.

For anyone who concentrates on the chosen field, progress could be faster. Here are some questions that will help you decide how fast and how far you have come.

1. What has been your success rate lately? If fewer than one in four of your queries lead to sales, I think you should press on for more

practice and greater skill at the magazine level.

2. How much material have you got in print? I suggest that you should wait until you have sold, piece by piece, at least the equivalent of an average book—say 75,000 words.

3. How fast can you write? Can you average 500 words of completely revised copy per day, and keep that up steadily, week after week, month after month? If you can, you should be able to handle the work of writing a book. There are several other questions you should consider.

## The Competition

What other books have already been written on the same subject? Probably you know some of them already. Check bookstores, your library catalog, and *Subject Guide to Books in Print* to find any that you've missed. It's worthwhile reading and analyzing each of them.

---

### Exercise 4:1

For each book on your subject, note these points:

Who is the publisher?

How old is the book? (See whether any revisions have been made since the original publishing date.)

Who is the author? Has he written other books on the subject?

How would you rate him as an expert? Score 0 to 10.

How would you rate him for ability to communicate? Score 0 to 10.

Carefully note any defects—errors, omissions, skimpy treatment in parts or in whole, outdated material, etc.

What items or sections strike you as particularly good?

What corrections, additions, new material, or other improvements could *you* provide?

Do this for all the books you can find that might compete with yours. Don't begrudge the reading and note-taking involved. These notes will be valuable to you later.

---

## Your Readership

A sound rule is "Write with a rifle, not with a shotgun." In other words, keep in mind a precise description of your reader; be sure that every word is aimed *directly at that reader.*

I cannot emphasize this point too strongly! Many would-be authors see their books as vehicles of "self-expression." OK, write all the self-expressive material you like, but do it in the form of a diary. Don't expect to publish it. Try to understand your readers and write for *them,* to help them express themselves.

Don't, for the sake of showing how much you know, put chunks of advanced material into a book aimed at beginners; they won't understand it and won't be able to apply it.

Don't include elementary material in a book aimed at people who already know it. It will bore them; they will feel cheated. (This book, for example, is no place for elementary instruction in spelling, punctuation, and grammar.)

Don't clutter the script with items that may be interesting to you but which are not relevant to the purpose of the book. (For example, I could write a long and, to me, interesting story of how I came to be a writer. But that has nothing to do with this book.)

___

**Exercise 4:2**

For each of the books you analyzed in Exercise 4:1, answer these questions:

Exactly who is the book aimed at?

Sex?

Age group?

Financial status?

Educational level?

Prior knowledge of the book subject?

Just what might these readers get from the book?

___

I have before me a full-page magazine advertisement for a Time-Life series of how-to books on home repair and improvement. Four illustrations show a man and woman working together at wall painting, electric wiring, bricklaying, and installing a kitchen ventilator. They appear to be in their early twenties. The text implies that they own their own home.

Readers of the ad are invited to start by inspecting the volume, *Plumbing*, for fifteen days, free. Everyone who does so will get, free, a sixty-four-page book, *The Home Tool Kit*, which bears on its cover illustrations of a handsaw, a carpenter's level, a tape measure, and a hammer.

That tool kit book, by itself, shows clearly the readers' assumed level of knowledge and experience; they are people who do not yet own even simple hand tools, and who need instruction in using them.

___

**Exercise 4:3**

Now make a preliminary analysis of the readers you expect to reach with your book:

Sex?

Age group?
Financial status?
Educational level?
Prior knowledge of your subject?
To apply what you intend to teach in the book:
How much would it cost them?
What tools and materials would they need?
How much space would it require?
How much time would it take?
Exactly what benefits will they get from applying your teaching?

## Defining Your Subject

You should have a precise definition of your subject before you start any serious planning. Confusion at this stage can waste a lot of time for you later on. Here are some hints.

### Not Too Big

Don't try to cover *the whole* of any subject in one book.

In the previously mentioned Time-Life series, the publisher does not try to teach beginners all about home repair and improvement in one volume. Plumbing makes one whole book. Other volumes in the series cover other subjects: Floors and Stairways, Basic Wiring, Masonry, Heating and Cooling, Roofs and Siding, etc.

Yesterday I was looking over a big rack of current how-to books in a local store. I jotted down some typical titles.

*Bookshelves and Cabinets.* Note that the book is not *Basic Woodworking* or even *Build Your Own Furniture,* but a whole book devoted to one branch of furniture making!

*Remodeling Kitchens* was next to it. There's another specialized subject.

The cookery section has a whole book on *Breads and Rolls,* one on *Soups and Stews* and another on *Cooking for Two.*

In this book, I'm not trying to say *all* about "writing"; I'm taking one narrowly defined aspect of the subject. Look at the title list of Writer's Digest Books: see how many of them deal with specialized subjects—Confessions, Interviewing, Short Stories, Greeting Cards, History, Poetry, Outdoor Writing, and so on.

Many book buyers prefer moderate-sized, moderate-priced books that contain exactly what they want to know. To be sure, there are still some books being written that aim to cover a whole subject— gardening, cookery, indoor games, sexual relations, etc.—in one volume. But such a thick, wide-ranging work represents a massive expenditure for a publisher; he might be reluctant to take such a gamble on a new writer. The beginner probably stands a better chance of acceptance with a less extensive project.

## Not Too Small

Yet you should also consider the question, "Is this really a *book-sized* idea?"

For example, this idea that I'm writing on now—"What constitutes a book-sized subject?"—is all right for one section of this chapter. It could make a worthwhile magazine article, or a short radio talk. But if, by windy writing and a surfeit of examples, I puffed it up to full book length, a reader would feel cheated—if he even bothered to finish it.

So think of those readers whom you have carefully defined. Ask yourself such questions as:

"Will this subject, written up to book length, give them an *interesting, prolonged* reading experience, *rich* and *varied* enough to make them feel they've received good value for their money?"

"Will this subject, treated as I mean to treat it, *add substantially* to the knowledge, skill, and personal satisfaction of those readers?"

## Personal Judgment

You must answer those questions, with regard to your subject, your knowledge of it, and your writing abilities. Any publisher to whom you submit your proposal will be thinking much along those same lines. So you may as well be honest with yourself at this preliminary stage.

I recommend that you take some time over the decision. Write notes about it; review them and revise them, over several days. Then, when you're fully satisfied, make a concise statement of the aim of your book. Say in one sentence exactly *what* the book is meant to teach or explain, and to *whom*.

My subject definition for this book was "This is primarily a workbook for writers who want to master the how-to form."

Note the expression "workbook." Description, commentary, criticism concerning how-to writing—I include all those. But they must be subordinate to the main concept. I intend, by offering a lot of exercises, to set readers *writing*. I keep that purpose in mind all the way through. I keep saying to myself, "Hull, it's not enough to ex-*plain* this point or that; you must make them *apply* it."

---

## Exercise 4:4

Write your one-sentence subject definition. Keep revising it until you are satisfied with it.

Type this definition on a slip of paper and stick it or hang it where you will see it all the time you are working on your book. It will continually stimulate your mind to produce the ideas you need. It will save you time and effort by preventing you from writing material that is not strictly to the purpose.

---

**Exercise 4:5**

Here is another way to learn from the Exemplary Dozen. For each one, check to see if the author has kept to one precisely defined subject.

If so, write out the relevant one-sentence subject definition.

With that definition in mind, analyze the various features of the book—descriptions, explanations, anecdotes, exercises, illustrations, etc. How well, or how poorly, does each item fit in with the main purpose?

---

## The Writer as Prophet

In your how-to writing realize that there is, between you and your readers, a distance not only of space, but of *time*, too! If you are writing for a weekly paper, the delay may be just a few days, but for a monthly magazine the delay will be several months; with a book, it may be as much as two years before the first copy reaches the public.

Moreover, some of your research may date back a long time prior to the moment of writing. (I have sometimes researched three or four years before starting a book.) So you must face the question "How much, if any, of my material will seem outdated or wrong by publication date?"

In subjects where new procedures and new materials are being rapidly developed, where costs are changing fast, where contests and exhibitions are often being held, where new stars are rising fast and old stars often setting, that question must seriously concern magazine and book writers alike.

But the book writer has another problem. He naturally wants to see his book stay in print and continue earning royalties for as long as possible. So he must ask "Will my material seem timely enough, be accurate enough, to keep my book selling for three, five, or ten years?"

A thorough knowledge of your subject will enable you to answer such questions. The listing of current world's records in any activity, for example, is best left to those almanacs that are reprinted annually. Such figures should not be used in books that are intended to have a longer life.

So be alert. If you see that some cherished tidbit of fact or opinion could be the item to make a whole book obsolete, be cold-blooded and omit it.

## What's to Come?

Here is a potentially more valuable manifestation of prophetic power. Can you predict, early enough, one or more of those "waves of interest" in various subjects that occasionally capture the public's attention?

Publishers are constantly trying to do that; but you can get in on the act. Be aware; try to sense the first faint stir of interest in some new subject, or in some long-neglected aspect of an old subject. Is that interest going to rise? When will it peak? Six months, a year, two years from now?

With your specialized knowledge of some subject or subjects, you have an advantage over the typical publisher. So listen, with the detective's ear, to people talking; watch, with the detective's eye, what they are buying. Thoughtfully analyze the correspondence columns of relevant papers and magazines. In particular, take note of the "Why doesn't someone . . ." kind of complaint, which usually indicates an unsatisfied curiosity.

When you find the clue, your carefully acquired fluency will be useful. You can quickly draw up the article query or the book proposal, get it accepted, and quickly write the script in time to have it out just when public interest is rising fast.

# The Outline

Now comes the task of developing that well-defined idea into a salable mass of words on paper. Begin by writing an outline. Imagine that you received a letter from a friend who asks, "What's this new book project of yours?"

How would you reply?

---

### Exercise 4:6

Draft an outline (300 to 350 words) of your book. Give the title; define your readership; summarize what you intend to put into the book; and say what it will do for those who utilize it.

If it's appropriate, briefly mention any inadequacies of existing books on the subject, and say how yours will fill the gaps.

Include in this outline a brief description of your qualifications: (a) what you know and have accomplished in the subject area; (b) your qualifications to write about the subject, e.g., other books or articles written, experience in teaching the subject, etc.

Lay the draft aside overnight, then revise it the next day. (A night's rest will give you a fresh perspective on the material.) If necessary, keep on rewriting till you have it just right.

Don't skimp on this exercise. Careful rewriting at this stage will pay big dividends. The outline will clarify your thinking about the book; it will help you to write the book; and it will be a valuable tool for getting the book sold and published.

Between revisions of the outline you need not sit twiddling your thumbs; you can get on with the chapter plan.

---

# The Chapters

As a matter of convenience for readers, it's customary to divide books into chapters, each chapter covering one section or aspect of the subject and each with its own title. Then, in rereading and practically applying the book, a reader can easily find and concentrate on those aspects that particularly interest him and can ignore the others.

So, from the start, begin to think of the book as something like a confederation of chapters, each serving its own function and contributing its share to the success of the whole.

## Main Chapter Subjects

Just how you go about this next stage of the work depends on how much you already have on paper.

1. Suppose you have gathered, over months or years, a mass of written and printed material—notes, clippings, photocopies from books and magazines. You may have photographs and sketches for possible use as illustrations. You may have tape-recorded material from interviews or off the air.

This or something like it is, I think, the best way to prepare for book writing, and I shall be saying more about the method in Chapter 11, "Research."

If you have a lot of such material, spend plenty of time looking it over and sorting it into piles, each dealing with one aspect of the subject. This procedure will give you ideas for chapter subjects.

While sorting, keep referring to your outline from Exercise 4:6. Don't hesitate to lay aside any of the raw material that is not relevant to the purpose of the book. Do this even if it hurts. Resist the temptation to tell all you know in one book. Anyway, some of the material discarded now may serve for writing magazine articles or another book.

Carefully consider what should be the order of these chapter subjects. Apply the general principle of beginning from what your readers already know and then proceeding in some logical order—chronologically through the stages of some process, from easy projects to difficult, or whatever seems appropriate.

2. Suppose you have little or no material on paper. You can get

started on this chapter planning by asking yourself "What are the main steps that I'm advising in order to fulfill the purpose of my book, as defined in Exercise 4:4?"

Here's another way to think of it: "Suppose I had to teach this subject in a night school. The students would be people much like my projected readers. I would have ten to fifteen sessions in the term. What ground would I cover in each session?"

Or perhaps you can review the stages by which you learned the subject yourself.

### Auxiliary Material

A chronological order of chapters may, as I said, be the best for some subjects—vegetable or flower gardening, winemaking, physical culture, etc. With such subjects, consider the value of a separate, short calendar chapter, summarizing all the procedures in proper order and at the right intervals.

Would your book be improved by a chapter with headings and spaces where the reader can write in his own records? For example, a wedding-organization book might have a chapter where the bride can record invitations sent out, gifts received, dates of acknowledgment, etc.

Chapter 16 of this book gives you space to record your progress with the exercises.

With some subjects, a chapter for financial accounts might be welcome, providing space for the reader to record the costs of equipment, materials, etc., and the income from sale of finished products.

---

### Exercise 4:7

Make a preliminary list of chapter subjects; arrange them in order.

---

## Chapter Summaries

Once you have defined your chapter subjects, you can draft a summary of what's going to be in each chapter.

Now you are getting down to the meat and potatoes of book planning. Sometimes, as you work on the summaries, your thoughts and words may expand into what will obviously be parts of the actual script. Capture these precious nuggets, but file them separately. Don't let the chapter summaries get too wordy.

---

### Exercise 4:8

Draft chapter summaries for your book.

As examples of this process, I will give a sample from the first draft of my chapter-by-chapter synopsis for this book.

How to Write How-to Books

### Chapter 1. The How-to Book

Describe its origins and growing importance for writers, readers, and publishers. Figures of various subject groups; relative popularity, etc. Future trends in the how-to field.

For successful writing, two basic components:

1. Expert knowledge.

(a) You are already an expert on the subject, and you are a capable writer. You write the book; you take all the credit.

(b) You are not already an expert; but by research, interviewing, experimenting, buying information, etc., you become an expert. You write the book and take all the credit.

(c) Collaboration. You work with someone else who provides the expert knowledge. You do the writing; both share the credit.

(d) Ghostwriting. Someone else provides the expert knowledge; you do all the writing; you get no credit.

Pros and cons of the various methods from the writer's point of view.

2. Writing technique. A special style required: not just describing, but teaching. Show the necessary elements of this style (with examples, of course).

### Chapter 2. Choosing the Subject

Timeliness: effects of fads and fashions; allowing for inevitable time delays in writing and publishing. Assess potential readership in two years' time.

Study the competition (i.e., other books on the subject). How many? How old? How good? What defects? What extra can you offer?

Even for the expert writing on his own subject, the choice may not be obvious, e.g., precisely define readership—beginner, intermediate, advanced, etc. Whom to aim at? How much to put in one volume? What prospects for sequels?

### Chapter 3. Selling Books

Explain customary selling procedures, for the beginning writer and for writers who have done short pieces but no books.

Studying the market; finding suitable publishers. The query: describe what preliminary work is needed; give query format, etc. The sample section. Possible negotiations before a decision. The contract.

Writing the script (describe format). Editing and revisions, where required. Proofreading.

General hints for smooth dealings with editors and publishers.

### Chapter 4. Research

Research methods for book writing: interviews; clippings; reading; experiments; questionnaires; surveys; night school and summer school courses; building a library.

The long-term approach to book research: gradually preparing for a number of books over the years. Keep putting in new subject ideas at one end as finished books emerge at the other.

Special research for how-to material: testing it on nonexperts. Can they understand? Does it seem practical?

A first-class method, if there's time: using script sections as texts in teaching a course.

### Chapter 5. Collaboration

How to act for best results in various collaborative setups.

(a) A nonwriter finds you and asks you to collaborate.

(b) You, as writer, seek a collaborator.

Hints on how to assess collaborators: what to look for and what to avoid.

Fairly assessing what each party contributes. Preliminary written agreements (sample texts given). Various working methods—face-to-face, by mail, by phone, etc.

Explaining the whole book business to the nonwriter collaborator. I've found this very important.

Handling personal and temperamental problems, e.g., unreliability, tantrums, jealousy, threatened lawsuits, suicide, etc. Dealing with the nonwriter who wants to meddle with the writing.

### Chapter 6. Illustrations

Illustrations often important for how-to books. Plan in advance what's required: drawings, plans, photos, black-and-white or color. Estimate this in your query to publisher.

Avoid amateur artwork! Only professional work will do. Finding good artists, photographers; keep a file on them.

Sample artwork with sample section to publisher.

Firmly settle means of paying artist. Written contract needed, specifying flat fee, paid by you (advance and installments) or share in advance and royalties from publisher. Estimating fair shares for artists.

Checking proofs of illustrations—very important!

### Chapter 7. Promotion

Author, and collaborator if there is one, can help sales of book.

Practical hints on various methods.

(a) Recommending possible sources for reviews.

(b) Newspapers, magazines, self-written material.

(c) Giving interviews to writers for the press.

(d) Broadcast media: detailed hints for effective interviews—exhibits, demonstrations, etc.

(e) Lecturing and teaching on the book subject.

(f) Long-term personal promotion with leaflets, etc.

You will notice that this synopsis covers only part of the material that eventually went into the book. That is normal; a first draft is necessarily rough. Still, the chapter subjects thus far noted are handled in a fairly detailed, orderly way. It's a useful beginning.

I suggest that you go on, finish reading this book, then turn back and look at that first draft synopsis again. You will see more clearly how, by rethinking and rewriting, an author develops a book from his original concept of it.

## Chapter Titles

While working on the chapter summaries, you can begin to create the chapter titles—preferably short ones. Nowadays long chapter titles are out of fashion. At one time, a lengthy title plus a five-line or six-line subtitle provided a summary of the chapter contents and a bait for the reader's curiosity or greed, something to make him read on. But at present that's taboo.

A writer showed me the first draft of a cookbook in which Chapter 1 was titled "The Language of Cookery and a Simple Glossary of Frequently Used Terms."

That's too long! Just those four words "The Language of Cookery" would be better.

The last chapter of the same book was originally titled "Whither Cookery in the Future, Some of Which Is Already Here?"

Again, too long! "Cookery in the Future" or even "Whither Cookery?" would have been better.

Another thing: Beware of the temptation to be clever in chapter titles. The pun, joke, or quotation, the bit of Greek, Latin, or French, may seem very funny to you; but perhaps it won't be clear to every reader. A good chapter title must convey its meaning *immediately* and *unmistakably*.

---

**Exercise 4:9**

Draft concise, meaningful titles for your chapters.

---

## Let Yourself Go

In the first stages of this chapter planning, don't hold yourself in, carefully weighing every idea, every word before you set it on paper. Stir the ideas up! Get them flying! In this, as in other aspects of writing, the first major task must be to get a rough draft, somehow, on paper.

So you can't think of the perfect way to write a line? Then write it imperfectly, with the knowledge that you can come back later and polish it up.

## Illustrations

Will your book need illustrations? That question must be decided early in your planning. Illustrations sometimes help to sell books. You have seen people in bookstores flipping over pages and studying the illustrations.

Yet, for many how-to subjects, illustrations are not necessary. My own *How to Get What You Want*, Napoleon Hill's *Think and Grow Rich*, Rudolph Flesch's *The Art of Plain Talk*, and umpteen others get along perfectly well with no photographs or diagrams. These books do not deal with the shaping or joining of physical objects; the procedures described need no special tools or equipment.

My suggestion would be, if a book does not positively demand illustrations, then do without them.

### The Question of Cost

But why not load up your book with scores or hundreds of beautiful illustrations, even though Raymond Hull, or some other adviser, says they're not necessary?

The reason is that illustrations add to the cost of books. *Cost*—it's a subject that many would-be writers of books have never considered. But cost sharply affects the behavior of the average reader. If he feels that a book is too expensive, he won't buy it. The publisher's aim is to produce books that will sell. If a proposed book seems too expensive to produce, he will not accept it.

Printing techniques and costs are changing fast, so any dollars-and-cents figures I quoted would likely be out of date before you read them. But here are some general remarks.

By far the most expensive illustrative arrangement is "full color, random pages." That means color illustrations are scattered irregularly through the book, each one adjoining the relevant passage in the text.

Colored illustrations printed in groups—usually 8, 16 or 32 pages together—are less expensive. Here, of course, it can be only a rare lucky accident that places an illustration facing its relevant text.

Black-and-white photographs are cheaper to print, and can often be placed just about anywhere you want them to go. With some printing processes, one extra color can be added to photographs at a moderate extra cost.

Black-and-white line diagrams in a book often cost no more to print than would the same space filled with words. With diagrams, too, it may be possible to add one color fairly cheaply. But bear in mind that someone has to pay for creating those diagrams; they don't come flowing out of a machine, as words come pouring out of your typewriter. Even if you can draw them yourself, you pay in time; if someone else draws them, you probably have to pay in money.

An illustrated book, even under the best conditions, will give you more trouble than a book of the same length without illustrations. The extra trouble may be anything from a few pinpricks to an avalanche!

I describe some of the problems in Chapter 13. You should take that extra trouble into account when making your decision for or against illustrations

### What Kind of Illustrations?

Suppose you have decided that your proposed book must have illustrations. You begin to ask, "What kind of illustrations will be most interesting and most helpful to my readers?"

A photograph shows the outer appearance of an object—the curves and curlicues but not the posts and beams, the skin and cloth but not the skeleton, the paint and lacquer but not the wood or steel. The camera sees, and reproduces well, lights and shadows, colors and textures. But it cannot discriminate between the trivial and the essential.

A diagram (the Greek roots of the word mean "through drawing") can show what's beneath the surface of an object and can show two, three, or four sides of it at once. A diagram is an abstraction; it can show certain features or qualities of the thing it represents and omit all that is irrelevant.

A diagram can exaggerate, for clarity, one or more features that are important in the text. Scale diagrams can show dimensions more easily and clearly than photographs.

### Estimating

Bearing in mind the points I have mentioned, begin to estimate how many and what sort of illustrations each chapter will require. How many are enough? I cannot tell you; you know your subject, and you know the problems of teaching it.

*Total Fitness in 30 Minutes a Week* by Laurence E. Morehouse and

Leonard Gross contains seven line drawings. Fred Reinfeld's *How to Play Chess Like a Champion* contains 125 diagrams and five cartoons.

See in writers' directories what various publishers say about their policies on illustrations. Bear in mind, too, that illustrations and words tend to balance each other—the more illustrations, the fewer words should be needed to fill the book.

## Total Wordage

How many words should your book contain? Maybe that sounds something like "How long is a piece of string?" but it's not really that vague. There is an optimum length for your book, and the sooner you can figure it out, even approximately, the better. Once you have a book contract, your publisher will tell you the length he wants your manuscript to be. But at this initial planning stage, you would do well to be guided by successful writers in your own field.

---

**Exercise 4:10**

Take three of the most recent books from those you analyzed in Exercise 4:1.

(a) Estimate what proportion of the total space is taken up by illustrations in each one.

(b) Estimate to the nearest thousand the number of words in each.

Now bear in mind that, for good financial and technical reasons, a publisher is probably not going to make your book very different in format from other similar books. Yours will have about the same total page area as others like it; it will be printed in a type size not much different from those other books; and it will probably require about the same proportion of illustrative space as has proved effective with others.

---

**Exercise 4:11**

Assuming that your book will be about average for its type in size and thickness:

(a) Estimate what proportion of your total space will be required for illustrations.

(b) Estimate to the nearest 2,000 the number of words it will contain.

You may be able to make a check of your estimate by studying writers' directory listings of firms that publish books similar to yours. Some publishers list minimum and maximum numbers of words or pages that they want. Some publishers say "length open"; some make no reference to length.

## Revising the Draft

The outline and the chapter summaries are going to need a lot of rewriting before you have them perfect. Here are some ideas that will help you in this revision:

1. Have you put in anything that is not necessary, or that would impair the total effect of the book?

I'll refer again to that cookbook draft. The original Chapter 10 was titled "Vegetarianism." The summary began, "I am not equipped to advise on vegetarianism, but there are many who are interested in eating in this fashion, at least part of the time. . . ."

I told the author that, since the great majority of her recipes included meat or fish, vegetarians were not going to buy her book anyway. So why bring up the subject at all? (Here's an example of failure to define the readership!)

Perhaps er totals add up to the book total that you determined in Exercise nism chapter, and begin by confessing that you don't know much about it. This approach will not impress a publisher; and even if it gets by the editor's blue pencil, it will not impress a reader! An old Chinese proverb says, "Don't point out the hole in the carpet; put your foot on it."

2. Can you improve the *order* of the chapters, so as to facilitate the reader's understanding and practical application of what you are offering? Deficiencies in the order of unfolding information are the largest single cause of editorial exasperation—and of readers' confusion and disappointment—in how-to books. So don't skimp on time and thought in reviewing this point.

Try laying out all your chapter files in order on a big table. See if physically moving them around will improve the order. As you handle each file, keep thinking:

"What does this item demand to have *before* it, so that the reader will understand—so that the reader will be *physically able* to perform whatever it is?"

"What does this item seem to *lead on to* next, so that the reader can advance easily and enjoyably?"

It would be a great help, at this stage, if you could get the material checked by two or three other people.

(a) It's good to hear from one person who knows nothing of the subject. Make it clear that all you want from him is an opinion of the *order*: does that seem clear and sensible to him?

(b) It's also useful to get some comments from an expert in your chosen subject and/or an experienced book author. Again, ask principally for his advice on this vital point of *order*. Make a point, also, of asking, "Is there anything important that you think I've left out?"

You may get such expert advice free, if you're lucky; but don't begrudge paying for it, if you have to, just as you'd pay a plumber or TV repairman for services rendered.

3. What about reader involvement? I've seen some supposed how-to books that contained much description and illustration of things the *author* had done and not many projects or exercises for the *reader* to do. Your chapter synopses should clearly show that you are offering plenty of things for the reader to do or make.

4. What about the illustrations? This is too early a stage to make full lists of illustrations. But have you given at least a rough idea of how many and what kind of illustrations each chapter will need?

5. Have you left out anything that should have been included? Keep trying to set yourself in the chair of your previously defined reader. Keep reminding yourself, "Many things that may be tediously familiar to me will be new and wonderful to my reader. Many things that I and my fellow experts do automatically will have to be explained, one step at a time."

6. At this stage, too, carefully review the proposed title of your book.

(a) Is it too long?

(b) Is it easily comprehensible? Remember, the typical customer in a bookstore or the reader of a publisher's advertisement skims rapidly over the titles displayed. Any that are not instantly understood will be passed over.

(c) Is it easy to pronounce? Remember that the most valuable publicity is by word of mouth. If a reader is not sure how to pronounce the title, he will be reluctant to talk about the book.

## Summary

Carefully study competitive books.

Analyze your proposed readership.

In one sentence, define the subject of your book.

Write an outline of your book in about 300 words.

Divide your material into chapter subjects.

Write a summary of each chapter.

Open a separate file for each chapter.

Plan the total wordage of the book.

Allocate wordage to each chapter.

Plan plenty of practical work for readers.

Keep rewriting the chapter summaries; they will be your representatives in dealing with publishers.

# 5

# The Proposal

A man who wanted to write a big, controversial nonfiction book asked my advice. I explained the usual procedure, but he took no notice; he was going to do it his way. He hammered out a script and mailed it to a publisher, who soon sent it back with a rejection slip.

The eager author promptly packed his bags and flew off to New York to deliver the script in person to the same publisher. "I *know* he'll buy it," said the writer, "if only I get the chance to explain it to him."

The personal explanations were in vain. The writer stayed in New York for weeks, hawking his script to the few publishers who would see him.

Several years later, the book remains unpublished. That man had overlooked one principle basic to all forms of writing: A script must speak for itself.

No publisher of books, magazines, plays, or anything else wants a script that depends on the author's verbal explanations to convey its message. Moreover, publishers of nonfiction books, as a rule, do not want to see unsolicited book scripts.

## First You Sell It

Would-be novelists generally have to write their books first and then try to find publishers. They are working against long odds. Some publishers buy only one in five thousand of the unsolicited novels they receive.

But nonfiction book writers, carefully using the procedures described in this book, can show a success rate of one in two and maybe better than that!

You sell a nonfiction book not by means of a complete script, but by a *proposal*. That's how, in the good old days, a lad would sell matrimony to a lass. He described to her the joys of married life, and his conduct during courtship gave her—supposedly—a sample of his future behavior as a husband.

You, as author, must propose not to romantic lasses, but to hard-bitten book publishers.

As I said in Chapter 2, some writers waste time and money in approaching the wrong publishers. Quite likely they feel, "That firm has a famous name. I'd like to be on their list of authors."

But that is not the right way to proceed. Don't think "Who would I like to sell to?" Look at the transaction the other way around: "Who is most likely to want the product I am offering for sale?"

## Which Publisher?

Each publishing house has a *policy*; that is, it has decided what kind or kinds of books it wants to publish. Publisher A, for example, may specialize in romantic fiction aimed at young women; Publisher B may publish nothing but inspirational books aimed at members of one religious denomination; Writer's Digest Books issues how-to books for writers.

You may assume that nothing you write, say, or do will make a publisher change his policy. Suppose you write a masterpiece on *How to Make Papier-Maché Fashion Ornaments*. Neither A nor B nor Writer's Digest Books is going to accept it; and no amount of persuasive letter writing, arguing by phone, or personal calling at the publisher's office will alter that fact!

Publishers do a certain amount of scouting for authors and book subjects, by reading magazines and by sending editors out to speak at writers' conferences, for example. But you must not just sit waiting to be discovered. Especially if you are new to book writing, it's you, the author, who must do the scouting and make the initial contacts with publishers.

From Exercise 4:1 you have some publishers' names. But you can probably find more in writers' directories—annual books that list, among other features, book publishers' names, addresses, and policies. Here are a few hints on interpreting the necessarily brief listings in those directories.

The publishers that use the phrase "how-to" are obvious prospects. But there are other policy expressions that might also indicate an interest in how-to material. Look for such listings as "health," "technical," "recreation," "hobbies," "do-it-yourself," "business skills," "management techniques," "self-reliance," etc.

---

**Exercise 5:1**

Make a list of publishers who might be interested in your book. For each publisher on the list, try to look over at least a few of his recently published books. Perhaps you already own some. You may care to buy a few more. You can see others in your library, and in bookstores.

Look at them critically. Publishers are not all alike. From the samples of his work that you see, try to size up each publisher. Those authors already on his list: what do you think of them, as technical experts, as writers? Would you want to be associated with them?

The favored style in his books: could you, or would you care to, write like that?

What do you think of the publisher's policy with regard to illustrations?

Are there other features of the books that impress you favorably or unfavorably?

Take your time. Think carefully; and give some weight to your feelings, as well as to your intellect. Remember, you are contemplating a *very big business deal*—a deal much more troublesome to get into, and quite likely longer-lasting, than a lot of marriages.

---

## The Proposal Format

Some technical elements of the writer's trade—the paper size, the typewriter, the double-spacing, etc.—are unshakably fixed. But on the question of how to make the most effective book proposal, there are some differences of opinion. I will describe what I have found to be a good method, and I will point out a few ways in which the procedure may be varied.

Remember how, earlier in this chapter, I defined a *proposal: a detailed description* of the product you are offering, plus a *sample* of it. So here, for your book proposal, are the items to prepare.

### Letter

This, in ordinary single-spaced business letter format, should be quite brief. Just put something like "Would you be interested in my book *So-and-So?* Here is an outline of the book and a sample of the script. This is [or is not] a simultaneous submission."

It would do no harm to give your phone number, including area code, with your mailing address, in case—happy thought—the editor wants to reach you in a hurry.

N.B. Even if other items in your proposal are photocopies, this letter should, as a point of courtesy, be a typed original throughout.

## Exercise 5:2

Write your proposal letter.

## Title Page

This separate sheet shows what the title page of your proposed book will look like. In the top left-hand corner type your name and address; about one-third of the way down, centered, the title of your book. Four spaces below that, centered, type your name in whatever form you want to have it used for publication.

## Exercise 5:3

Prepare your title page.

## Outline

This and all following items of your proposal should be in proper double-spaced script format. On a fresh sheet headed "Outline" type out a copy of Exercise 4:6. The main purpose of this outline is to let a publisher see at a glance if this is the sort of book that the firm wants.

## Exercise 5:4

Make a clean copy of your outline.

## Synopsis

Starting on a fresh sheet, give a chapter-by-chapter synopsis of the book. The material from Exercises 4:8 (chapter summaries) and 4:9 (chapter titles) will serve you here. At the end of the synopsis say how many and what kind of illustrations the book will need.

## Exercise 5:5

Make a clean copy of your chapter-by-chapter synopsis.

## Sample Section

This consists of a fair-sized chunk—somewhere from 5,000 to 10,000 words—written exactly as you want it to be in the book. It will give the publisher a good idea of your ability to explain and teach the proposed subject material.

　　Here are a few details for the layout of this sample: A chapter number and title go about one-fourth of the way down the page, each centered, but not underlined.

### Chapter 5
### The Proposal

Then, in order to divide the text into convenient parts, you use subheads and sub-subheads, like this:

### Subheads

Four spaces after the end of the previous section, type the sub-head, centered on the page but not underlined. Four spaces farther down, begin to type the wording of the text.

### Sub-Subheads

Four spaces after the end of the previous section, type the sub-sub-head at the left margin, not underlined. Four spaces farther down, begin the text.

Now, what exactly is to be offered as that so-important sample? "Obviously, begin at the beginning," you may think.

But, especially with how-to writing, the first chapter, or even the first two chapters, may not be truly representative.

Perhaps Chapter 1 describes the history and development of some art or craft; then Chapter 2 describes present-day materials and apparatus and tells where to get them. Such information is good and necessary, but still may not show whether the author really can teach *how to do* whatever the book is about.

(a) Some publishers, in their directory listings, positively demand to see the first two chapters; then that's what you'll have to send.

(b) Some publishers ask for Chapter 1 plus one other chapter that the author thinks is truly representative of the book.

(c) Some publishers will look at *any* two chapters which, in the author's judgment, are a fair sample of what he has to offer.

(d) Some publishers say they want one truly representative chapter.

So what's to be done? All through your planning, researching, and other preparatory work, keep at the back of your mind the thought, "I shall eventually want to offer an impressive-looking sample!" Now and then review what you've done and think what would best represent your writing and your subject.

My own inclination, for this sort of writing, would be to deal first with publishers who give at least some freedom in choosing sample material.

You need not send all the illustrations that belong to the sample section, but you should indicate in the script the place where each illustration is to go. Type a solid line clear across the page. Then briefly describe the subject and medium of the illustration. Give each illustration a number consisting of chapter number, a colon, and figure number. Double-space below the description, then put another line across the page. For example:

---

Figure 18:5
Line drawing: scale plan for parts of garden chair

---

If your book depends heavily on illustrations, you would be wise to include a few sample illustrations with your proposal, to show that you can in fact deliver the goods.

Each page in the whole proposal (except the letter) should be numbered. Numbers go in the top right corner of the sheets. In the top left corner of each sheet, except the title page, put a little code phrase, consisting of your surname followed by a slash and then one or two significant words from the title, e.g., for the sample and final script of this book, "Hull/How-To."

The value of the code phrase is that, if a batch of papers is accidentally scattered at the editorial office, all of yours can promptly be identified and reassembled.

The whole proposal, when typed and checked for accuracy, should be mailed in an envelope big enough that the sheets can lie flat. If the publisher's directory listing names one person as responsible for your type of book, then address it to that person.

Enclose another envelope, the same size, self-addressed, and bearing enough postage to bring the proposal back to you if it's rejected. Publishers' notices in writers' directories and magazines often use the abbreviation SASE to indicate that you are expected to provide such a "self-addressed stamped envelope."

---

**Exercise 5:6**

Write your sample section.

---

**Alternative Procedures**

(a) Some writers prefer to put the "Author" material (description of your qualifications) in the letter instead of at the end of the outline. I don't think it makes much difference.

(b) Some authors prefer to send, and some publishers will read, a query consisting of a letter plus the outline and synopsis described above, but no sample section. If you try this method, your letter should say something like: "Here is an outline and synopsis of my proposed book So-and-So. Would you be interested in seeing a sample section?"

It would be a good idea to have that sample section ready, or nearly ready, so that you can if need be deliver it with reasonable speed.

### Your Ambassador

Whatever material it contains, make sure that the whole proposal looks really slick! Those few sheets of paper represent you, not only by the words they carry but by the way they look. Remember, you are not the only fish in the sea. Other writers are bidding for places on each publisher's list. When the competition is keen, small details may decide the result.

## Summary

Approach only publishers whose catalogs include your kind of book.

Study publishers' listings of their own requirements.

The proposal format:
    An introductory letter
    A title page
    An outline
    A chapter-by-chapter synopsis
    Several thousand words of text
    Maybe some sample illustrations

Make your proposal look impressive.

# 6

# The Book Publishing Process

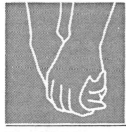

Book publishing is an industry with its own working methods, different from the methods of magazines, newspapers, film, radio, and television. It has its own customs and conventions. You will be expected to conform to those methods, customs, and conventions, so it is to your advantage to learn all you can about them.

**Exercise 6:1**

Get a big envelope or a shoe box. On it write BOOKS AND BOOK PUBLISHING. Systematically clip from newspapers and magazines every item you can find that refers to this subject. On each clipping write the date and the source. Thus you'll build a private, up-to-date reference file about the industry; thus you'll gain an increasing advantage over writers who don't have such information.

## The Exemplary Dozen

I'm a collector of how-to books. I keep giving them away to the library and to friends, but I always have about sixty on hand. The oldest dates back more than a century, and I keep buying new ones on subjects that interest me—especially writing, chess, health, personal development, and occult powers—as they come out.

Much of my writing is in the how-to field, so it makes sense for me to study the works of my competitors. Most artists and creative workers do this.

Yet some writers seem to think it is unnecessary. A woman once told me, "I'd like to be a writer, but I don't know where to begin."

"What do you read?" I asked her. I expected that the answer would show where her interests lay.

"I really don't care for reading," she replied. "I just want to write."

Don't be like that! I recommend that you make an extensive study of the how-to form.

Get a dozen how-to books. Some of them may tell how to do things that you have no desire to do. That doesn't matter. You are going to study this Exemplary Dozen not with the reader's but with the writer's eye! All of them are examples of successful how-to writing. They have found publishers and readers. That's what you want to do with your projected book or books.

Thus you can learn not only from me, but from a dozen other successful authors as well.

---

### Exercise 6:2

Get a dozen sheets of paper and on each write the title of one book and the names of its author(s) and publisher. (It's useful to form the habit of thinking of publishers in connection with books.)

Now make a start at understanding some technical details of this product.

Check the publishing history of each book. When was the first edition published, and by whom?

What reprintings, if any, of that edition have been issued?

Is yours a copy of the original edition? Or is it in some different format—say a paperback from a hardback, a translation, an adaptation, a condensation, an expansion, an anthology, etc?

For each book, estimate the number of words and the number of illustrations that it contains.

Are any other books by the same author, or by different authors, advertised in the book? If so, why were those titles selected for mention?

---

## Behind the Scenes

Let's look at the operations of an imaginary firm, Rayback Books, Inc. Rayback publishes how-to books on indoor games, outdoor sports, physical fitness, and character development.

Here, in Rayback's editorial department, they are looking through the morning's mail. Much of it is from writers already known to the firm, dealing with books now in process of production, or with books planned for the near future.

There's material from new writers, too. Some of this lands on the desk of Monica Markwell, one of the firm's six editors.

1. *The Ball Game*. A script, beautifully typed—750 pages of text, plus a lot of elegantly drawn diagrams. The foreword shows that the author aims to prove that the earth is not a ball, as is commonly believed, but a ring, something like a huge donut!

Whatever the scientific or literary merits of this script, it is not the sort of book that Rayback publishes, so there is no use looking further. Some publishers make a practice of keeping all submissions at least a month, so authors will think their scripts have been read right through. Rayback does not do that; so *The Ball Game* goes straight back to its author.

Such rejections usually carry a short printed form: "We regret to say that this script does not meet our needs at this time," or something like that. Editors don't have time, and publishers don't have money, to give detailed explanations for every rejection.

(N.B. There *are* publishers who handle books like *The Ball Game*. The author should have begun with one of them, instead of wasting postage and time by submitting to Rayback.)

2. *New Ways of Winning Backgammon* is a three-inch-thick bundle of pages. Backgammon, to be sure, is a popular game, and there may be some new ways of teaching people how to win. But this script is handwritten!

Ms. Markwell has to attend an editorial meeting tomorrow afternoon; she already has two good book ideas to bring forward for discussion. She would like to find a third; and someone has remarked that the "board games" section of the list is getting a little thin . . . still, 400 pages of handwriting! (A publisher's "list" is its catalog of books in print.)

As I said earlier, most firms simply send back handwritten scripts unread. Rayback doesn't do that. Nevertheless, this item must go to the bottom of the pile, until Ms. Markwell has time to read it—maybe next month, during her vacation.

3. Ah! Here's something! *Better Chess by Self-Conditioning*. First comes a brief explanation of the general purpose of the book—application of behavioristic training methods to improve one's chess skills.

The author explains his qualifications. Dwight Knight is a state chess champion, writes a weekly chess column for his hometown newspaper, and for the past five years has been teaching chess courses in night school. Two pupils from his classes have won junior regional championships.

A chapter-by-chapter synopsis shows the plan and contents of the book. A sample section of the script—the chapter on "Memory Development"—shows a clear, interesting style, and a clever use of exercises to help readers transform theory into practice.

Item 3 goes before the editorial committee. The members are impressed; this looks like the kind of book they want, and its author, perhaps, is the sort of writer who could do more books for them later.

This committee decision is not a final pledge to buy the book. It's the signal for Ms. Markwell to begin what may be a delicate process of negotiation, with a letter somewhat like this:

Dear Mr. Knight:
We are interested in your proposed book, *Better Chess by Self-Conditioning*, but we think some changes might improve it.
   [Here follows a list of possible changes to the plan and text.]
   Would you consider these suggestions? We think they would increase the sales potential of the book.

Sincerely yours,
Monica Markwell

Some conceited writer might take a letter like this as an insult. "How dare she criticize me like this?" he says to himself (or to his wife, or to members of his writers' club). "Doesn't she know that I'm an expert—a *great* expert—on my subject? Not one word, not one comma of my book is going to be changed! They can like it or lump it!"

Ms. Markwell does not like dealing with such arrogant, hostile people, and of course she has no way of forcing writers to make changes. So Rayback's interest in them and their work evaporates.

But chess champion Knight is a prudent man; and, especially since he is new to book writing, he recognizes the letter as a piece of instruction that he could not buy at any price. True, he is an expert on chess, but Ms. Markwell is an expert on book publishing. And Knight realizes that any book is a joint effort, an expression of the writer's talents and knowledge *plus* the personality, technical skill, and business ability of the publisher and his staff.

So he promptly writes Ms. Markwell that he will consider her suggestions, and will send in a revised proposal as soon as he can.

## How About You?

Suppose you are in a similar situation. You have received a preliminary expression of interest from a publisher. Perhaps, after careful thought, you find that one of the editor's suggestions is unacceptable. Then, when you send the revised proposal, you courteously explain why that particular thing should be left as it was. (In my book-writing career I've received a lot of suggestions from editors; a few I've declined, but most of them have indeed been helpful.)

One point is worth special mention. An editor will sometimes recommend a change in a book's title. From what I hear, there's nothing writers cling to more tightly than their titles! But the editor knows, or can quickly find out, the titles of all other books in the field. (There's no point in duplicating or coming embarrassingly close to some title that is already in another publisher's list.)

Through the sales department, she has a good idea of booksellers' and readers' reactions to certain title forms—even to individual words! So, on titles, the editor probably does know best, and the writer should yield as gracefully as he can.

There may be several such exchanges of correspondence, several revisions of the proposal, before a contract is offered. Through all this, try to maintain an interested, cooperative state of mind. You are learning—learning more about your abilities as a writer, and more about the book publishing business.

## The Contract

The contract is a legal instrument by which you give the publisher authority to print and distribute your book. Here are the main points to look for:

### Book Rights

This term means that you are selling the publisher exclusive rights to print and sell the book in whatever area the contract specifies—one country, several countries, or the whole world.

### Payment

An author's payment for book writing, called a "royalty," is usually calculated as a percentage of the retail price of the copies sold. Or it may be based on "net receipts" (the publisher's actual income after the discount the book is sold at). On hardback books, 10 percent is the usual base rate. If the book sells well, the author's royalty should rise, and the contract indicates the points—marked by thousands sold—at which the raises occur. A typical scale: 10 percent on the first five thousand; 12½ percent on the next five thousand; 15 percent on all sales above ten thousand.

For paperbacks, you might expect a royalty of 7½ percent or 8 percent, probably rising to 10 percent on sales above ten thousand and 12½ percent at some higher sales figure.

I haven't space to explain the economic and technical factors, but it is quite fair that paperbacks should yield lower royalty rates than do hardbacks. Anyway, a successful paperback may sell ten to twenty times more copies than the same book in hardback; so the author earns more in the end.

There will usually be an advance payment for the author—a thousand, or a few thousand dollars—payable by installments, maybe half on signing the contract and half later on, either when you deliver the full script or when the book is published. Bear in mind that this advance comes *out of your royalties.* The bigger the advance, the longer you must wait to start getting royalties from continuing sales.

Let me emphasize that I'm not citing any terms for royalties and advances as being the "right" ones. Various publishers may offer various scales. Some authors may have more and some less urgent need for advance payments. There may be scope for negotiation on these financial terms, but the first-book author is usually not in a strong negotiating position.

### Illustrations and Contracts

Illustrations, for many how-to subjects, are an essential part of the book. It's advisable to get a definite statement in the contract of what illustrations are required—approximately how many, and in what medium.

You, as author, are normally expected to provide all those illustrations, either by producing them yourself or by paying someone else to do so. The publisher will certainly reserve the right to judge the acceptability of the illustrations you provide, and to demand the redoing of any that are inadequate—artistically or technically—for reproduction.

There may sometimes be scope for negotiation: sometimes a publisher can supply some or all of the illustrations; sometimes he may be willing to share the cost. You can ask for some such deal; but don't build your hopes too high!

### Subsidiary Rights

This section specifies rates of payment for other uses of the material—for example, in translations, book clubs, films, or television. A common division of subsidiary rights earnings is 50 percent to the author and 50 percent to the publisher.

### Deadline

The contract sets a date for finishing the script. There may be sharp penalties, such as losing part of your advance, if you don't deliver on or before that date.

### Option

This means that you will let the publisher have first look at one or more of your future books. It is not a firm promise that he will buy; if he does not want the book, you are free to try to sell it elsewhere.

**Take Care!**

These notes are only a skeleton outline; the typical contract is much longer. Some contracts are several pages of fine print. Remember, a book contract is a major commitment for both parties; it is certainly a great expenditure of time and effort for you against—maybe—a lot of money. (It's not unknown for a single book to form the basis of a writer's reputation, and earn him revenue for tens or scores of years.)

So don't sign casually! I am not suggesting that your publisher is aiming to cheat you; but, if you are not sure that you understand everything in the contract, get advice from a lawyer. If you can find one who has experience with writers and publishing, so much the better.

## From Contract to Deadline

All through the writing of the book, which may take six months, nine months, a year, or more, the editor maintains watchful, tactful contact with the writer. Some writers get discouraged and lag behind schedule; they must be made to speed up. Other writers rush ahead too fast and turn in sloppy scripts that do not fulfill the promise of the proposal. They must be coaxed or bullied into doing the necessary rewriting.

What if some real, unexpected problem crops up—serious illness, for example—that would prevent your meeting the deadline? Don't just drift on, worrying, and let the deadline slip by with no finished script to deliver. *Immediately* notify your editor; perhaps some compromise can be made.

But don't keep pestering the editor, by phone or by mail, with your run-of-the-mill doubts, fears, little technical hitches, aches, coughs, and domestic problems! Editors are human beings. They tend to resent people who strain their patience and make the work excessively difficult. They tend to like people who are polite, cooperative, and dependable.

While she is watching the writer, the editor is also keeping an eye on the calendar, because in book publishing several different operations must be scheduled, interlocked, and done on time if the planned numbers of books are to be in the stores for sale by the desired date.

Here are some of those operations:

**Design.** The design department is planning how best to fit the proposed numbers of words and illustrations into some appropriate shape and size of book. They are also designing the title page, binding, and jacket, probably in consultation with the sales department.

**Production.** Contrary to what many writers think, very few publishers have their own printing presses and binderies. All the same, the publisher has to buy the paper for the book. So the production department is estimating how much and what kind of paper will be needed, and is ordering it well ahead of time. They are also getting estimates from two or three printers and binders. To help this estimating, they may ask the author to submit a few sample illustrations ahead of time.

**Publicity.** This department is writing text for the inside flaps and back of the book jacket. They are gathering biographical information about the author for news releases and catalogs and for special, local-appeal publicity in his hometown. They may also be seeking radio and TV interview spots for the author.

**Advertising and Sales.** Working closely with Publicity, these departments are planning to bring the book to the attention of wholesalers, retail booksellers, and libraries who might want it, then to take orders and distributed the printed copies.

In some firms these functions may have different names and may be distributed differently; editors may take more or less active roles in them. But you may be sure that all these things are being done for ten, twenty, forty, or more books at the same time. So you, while sitting alone at the typewriter, are part of a very complex process! You should not expect to have all of an editor's thought and time. Your book, for the moment, occupies all *your* attention—quite rightly! But it's only one of many conflicting claims upon hers.

---

### Exercise 6:3

Clip from newspapers and magazines all examples you can find of advertisements for how-to books. Make a listing of phrases and words that reveal the publishers'—and presumably the readers'—thinking about such books. What values or qualities are emphasized—ease, simplicity, economy, profit, power, prestige, pleasure, health? See if this study helps you clarify your thinking about your own book. What values or qualities are you trying to emphasize? How clearly, how consistently, are you doing so?

---

### Exercise 6:4

Make a similar analysis of the descriptive material on the jackets or covers of the Exemplary Dozen. The publishers wrote all this; it helps you to understand them better.

## Copyediting

This is the part of an editor's work that most people associate with the verb "to edit"—that is, to condense, revise, or correct a piece of writing to make it fit for publication. Some publishing houses employ copyediting specialists; in others, the work is done by the general editors.

The editor's first task is to check the length of the script. Suppose your contract calls for 75,000 words, but you wrote only 65,000. The editor at once spots this deficiency, and dashes off a letter asking you to make it good, pronto.

A few hundred words too many she would be able to cut herself—ten here, twenty there, throughout the text. But suppose that, instead of 75,000, you overzealously wrote 85,000. Those 10,000 extra words would be unwelcome, like extra inches on the legs of a pair of pants. You would be asked to eliminate them somehow.

Big additions or big cuts, at this stage, would give you a lot of extra work, to be done in a rush. That's unpleasant! It's always best to deliver exactly what you contracted for—no more and no less.

The editor must check the script for errors in spelling—not so easy as it sounds! What about obscure technical and scientific terms for which there may be two or more different spellings in use? What about proper names? Maybe Mr. Knight's chess book refers to the nineteenth-century master sometimes as Kieseritski and sometimes as Kieseritzky. The editor is supposed to spot that discrepancy, find out which of the two spellings is better, and see that one form is used throughout.

She would have to watch the easy words as well. Some authors simply don't worry about spelling, and send in scripts splattered with mistakes. "Why worry?" they think. "The editor will correct them. What are editors paid for, anyway?"

In punctuation there may be room for discussion as to what is "correct"; but, without doubt, some methods are better than others for how-to writing. (I discuss that point in Chapter 12.) Anyway, whatever rules of punctuation may be adopted, they should be uniformly applied throughout the book, and the copyeditor must check that they are.

At this stage, too, the editor is watching for any problems that may arise later in typesetting—sizes of type that will be required, placement of heads and subheads, etc. Such things will strongly affect the appearance and usefulness of the finished book.

This first editing may raise in the editor's mind some questions of fact, style, possible rearrangement of material, etc. Such questions will be referred to you, with detailed notes of the sections of script involved. Answer the questions and make the alterations as fast as you can.

When the script is finally ready, it goes to be set in type.

## Proofs

A trial printing produces "galley proofs"—long strips of paper, each containing about enough material for two or three pages of the finished book. The editor looks over these and marks any noticeable errors; then they come to you for your checking. The publisher will probably send you detailed instructions for this job. If not, see the instructions in *A Practical Style Guide for Authors and Editors* by Margaret Nicholson.

In a how-to book, give special care to checking numbers in the text and on diagrams; also pay special attention to any other technicalities that printers and editors probably would not know about. The best way with difficult material is to get someone else to check it on the proof while you read it aloud, item by item, from your carbon copy of the original script.

Important! Don't seize on this proofreading as an opportunity for rewriting the script! Many book contracts specify that any corrections made by the author at this stage, exceeding 10 percent of the original typesetting bill, will be charged to the author and deducted from his royalties. The only justification for rewriting at this stage would be some brand-new discovery that has made part of the text wrong.

If some such correction becomes necessary, try to make the new material exactly the same length (i.e., the same total number of letters, figures, punctuation marks, and spaces) as the material that you have to delete. That way, you can save a lot of time and money for the editor and printers, and help build yourself a reputation as a careful, conscientious writer.

The galley proofs usually come with a reminder that the reading, and any corrections, should be done fast. Take that to heart; *do it fast,* and get those proofs back to the publisher as soon as you can.

Some time later, you may receive a thick bundle of "page proofs"; the corrected galley proofs have been divided into numbered sheets, the same size as the pages will be in the finished book. Such things as chapter headings, footnotes, illustrations, etc., are now in their proper places. You have to give these page proofs a final check for errors. (Some publishers' production schedules don't allow for page proof review by the author, so don't expect to receive them as a matter of course.)

If the previous stages have gone well, there should be no need for alterations on the page proofs. If you feel tempted to rewrite, check the section of the contract covering the penalties you will pay for alterations at this stage!

Read those proofs as fast as you can. If you feel you simply must show off to your family and friends, then rush the proofs by hand to a photocopying firm, who will gladly make you a reproduction of the whole set in a few minutes. Keep those photocopies for exhibition at your "proof party" and send the originals back to the publisher at once.

This two-stage proof system—galleys plus page proofs—has long been the accepted one; with many printers and publishers it will doubtless continue in use for years yet.

But some new computerized typesetting systems yield a preliminary set of proofs before the galleys. This "line proof"—or whatever term may be used for it—looks, in typeface and format, nothing like the finished book.

It is more like a typewritten copy of the edited script, printed on strips of paper several yards long. The text is adorned with umpteen letter codes, numbers, and symbols; these represent the editor's instructions for changes of typeface, spacing, punctuation marks, etc.

You need not bother yourself with all those code marks. You simply check the text for accuracy, mark any corrections, and ship the proofs back as fast as you can. Then those corrections will be fed into the computer that sets the type.

If you get such preliminary proofs, don't fret or fume. The work you put into correcting them reduces the work to be done later on the galleys; it saves precious time in this always-rushed stage of book writing.

Don't feel that you are being particularly put upon by all this hustle. Various people at the publisher's office—general editor, copyeditor, art editor, designer, and such—are also hurriedly checking, trying to be sure that the book, when in print, will do credit to you and to them.

## The Time Frame

Some beginning book writers get unduly anxious about the fate of their projects. At all stages, from the initial correspondence right up to publication date, they keep feeling neglected, fearing that they and their books have been forgotten. They keep firing off letters and phone calls, even making personal visits to publishers' offices, demanding, "What's the delay? Why haven't you answered my proposal?" "Why isn't my book ready yet?" and so on.

Such behavior does not speed up the book; it only makes the editor thoroughly sick of you; and it impairs your prospects of selling again to the same publisher.

If you decide to involve yourself with books, then realize that book publishing—for very good reasons—is a slow-moving business. Try to cultivate the virtue of patience; it will help to preserve your health, and it will help to make you more popular with publishers.

## Summary

Collect how-to books, and *study* them.

Occasionally put yourself in the editor's shoes.

Carefully consider editors' suggestions on proposals and scripts.

Don't be stubborn about book titles.

Be sure to understand a contract before you sign it.

Fulfill your end of the contract:

    Be businesslike.

    Deliver exactly what you promised.

    Meet the deadline.

Recognize the complexity of the publisher's business: be a help, not a hindrance.

Speed is important during copyediting and proofreading.

The book business moves slowly: be patient.

# 7

# How to Find a Collaborator If You're Not a Writer

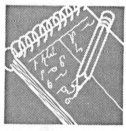 Do you have technical knowledge, experience, and exceptional skill in some specialty? Have you invented some mechanism, technique, or process that is new, better than anything previously used for the purpose? Are you a prizewinner, a champion in your field? Have you proven your ability to coach or instruct other people—one at a time or in groups—in some skilled activity?

If so, you have probably thought, and quite likely you have often been told, that your knowledge would be salable in book form.

Yet perhaps you don't want to take the time from your career that would be needed to become an expert writer. You prefer to keep on actively practicing your subject—making money, improving your skill in what you know you can do best.

But you can have both book and career, if you find a capable collaborator, a writer who can put into publishable form the technical knowledge you have at your fingertips.

## Problems

I should, in honesty, warn you that this kind of collaboration—technical expert with writer—is not always one smooth ride from initial idea to completed book.

Writers, in general, are not the easiest people to get along with. They tend to be egocentric and undiplomatic; some of them are unreliable; and it has often been said that the occupational disease of writers is alcoholism. Nevertheless, there are many good writers— that's the kind you want to find and deal with. And often a writer who's no angel will still possess that precious ability to transmit facts, ideas, actions, and feelings accurately and vividly, through space and time, by means of black marks on white paper.

Collaborative writing, as a rule, takes longer than the same amount of solo writing. And any writer worth his salt will want to be (and should be) well paid for the work he does on your behalf. If the book project succeeds, it will be well worth all you have invested. A successful book can earn you a lot of money; it can enhance your reputation in your own field of expertise; it can open doors to various lucrative, pleasurable activities—lecture tours, radio and television interviews—that you would never have enjoyed without it.

I am going to talk principally in this chapter about collaborative book writing. A professional writer would probably not want to bother collaborating on magazine articles; the earnings from an article, divided between the two of you, would scarcely pay for his time and trouble. I will begin by emphasizing that book writing is a *big, slow* procedure. It will probably take *at least two years* from the time you read this chapter, and decide to act upon it, before you see your book in print. Many books take longer than that.

This glacial rate of progress will not be your collaborator's fault. It inevitably follows from the size of the writing project itself, and from the established methods of the book publishing business. So be sure you are emotionally and financially prepared for long delays.

You will be required to sign contracts with your writer-collaborator and, later on, with a publisher. Such contracts commit you to a heavy expenditure of time, effort, and, quite likely, money too, for such things as costs of illustrations. You may be penalized for failure to fulfill the terms of the contracts.

## What Do You Have to Offer?

Before you make any move toward creating your own book, take time to analyze the books on your subject that are already available. You probably already own, or have read, some of them; but see if there are others you don't know about.

Look in the main book index of your public library, under the name of your subject. Look at the *Subject Guide to Books in Print.* Ask for information in the library department that includes your subject, and in stores that sell supplies and equipment for your subject.

Find all the relevant books that you can. This is your competition! So carefully analyze those books, making notes as you go.

(a) The books will help you compile a complete list of things that ought to go in your book.

(b) Look for things that other writers have omitted; plan how you would fill those gaps.

(c) Look for things in other people's books that you believe to be wrong. Note how you would correct those errors.

(d) Note any items that seem outdated, or that might be outdated soon. What's needed to bring such items up-to-date, and keep them up-to-date for at least the next few years?

(e) Study the illustrations that other writers have used. Carefully note which ones are good, so-so, and bad. Why? What subjects and what techniques of reproduction have been used—photography and/ or drawings and diagrams of various kinds? What improvement could you suggest?

(f) Pick out the book that you feel is the worst you've seen on the subject. Make a written list of the reasons why you dislike it.

(g) Pick out the book that you feel is the very best you've seen on the subject. Make a written list of the reasons why you like it. What could you offer to make your book even better?

Take a few days to review and think over all of this; then put down in writing—a couple of pages will be enough—some notes to show exactly what you want to achieve with your proposed book, and just how it would be more accurate, more comprehensive, or more up-to-date than existing books. Try to think of a good title for it.

Let's call these notes your *objective statement.* Get the objective statement typed out, and three or four copies made.

This preliminary research, and thinking and note making, is important. It will help you to get a good collaborator—because you will have, not just a vague idea, but some specific, partly organized material to offer. The preliminary work will also save time for you and the collaborator when you face the big task of making a detailed plan for the book.

## Choosing a Writer-Collaborator

Let's define more exactly what you should be looking for. I have used the term "writer," but there are about as many different kinds of writers as there are singers, painters, or musicians. Each may be well qualified in his own way; but none can do *every* kind of work within the whole range of his profession.

### What Kind of Writer?

(a) You need a successful *nonfiction* writer. Many poets, short story writers, and novelists, though successful in their own fields, would be unable to do the work you want. By "successful" I mean that the writer should have sold, and had published, some of his work—the more, the better. For such a big, important project, you had best not bother with beginners.

(b) Prior experience in *how-to* writing would be an asset. Someone who has written about history, politics, art criticism, etc., might not possess the particular touch and style that make for success in how-to subjects.

(c) Your best prospects for success would be with a collaborator already experienced in *book writing*. The step up from article writing to book writing is a big one. It's better, from your point of view, if the collaborator has already made that step on his own, instead of experimenting on you and your material.

These qualifications narrow down the field considerably. You may not be able to get all of them fulfilled, but they are what you should aim for.

### Writers, Writers, Everywhere

Lots of people go through life without ever meeting anyone whom they recognize as "a writer." Yet there are plenty of writers around, if you know how to find them.

(a) Keep your eyes open for news of local writers in newspapers and magazines—publication of new books, awards, contests, and such events.

(b) Phone or write whoever runs the book review sections of local newspapers or magazines.

(c) Ask in the Language and Literature section of your public library, and in local bookstores.

(d) Make contact with local writers' clubs. Libraries and community centers may have information about them and their activities. Some of them advertise public readings, lectures, etc.

(e) Check the night school and community college programs in your neighborhood; there are probably some writing courses advertised. The instructors of these courses will be writers.

(f) Check the writers of how-to columns or articles in your local papers and magazines.

(g) Track down some retired journalists; they should have retained the ability to write fluently and clearly.

(h) Check the Yellow Pages of your phone book under "Writers."

(i) Advertise. You can use the classified columns of local newspapers or the free notice boards of community centers, libraries, and supermarkets.

### Making the Choice

Your search may turn up several possible candidates. If so, interview them one at a time, preferably at your workshop, studio, home, or wherever you have some materials, products, etc., concerning your subject.

Here are some points to look out for:

(a) Check the candidate's qualifications, as described under "What Kind of Writer?"

(b) Does he show a businesslike attitude? Did he arrive for the appointment on time? Did he think to bring samples of his published work or other evidence of his qualifications? Did he bring writing materials to make notes of what is discussed?

This "businesslike attitude" is important! For a collaborative book, you will have many face-to-face meetings with the writer. If he often comes late, or forgets to come at all, there goes part of your day! If he's sloppy and unreliable in the heavy correspondence that will be required with publishers, there goes part of the credibility of your joint product—the book. If he misses the deadline for finishing the script, you also may be penalized.

The publisher must to a large degree judge *you*, your knowledge and your skill, through the medium of the writer you have chosen to work with.

(c) Show the candidate your objective statement. Talk to him about your subject; demonstrate some practical aspect of it, if you can. Does he seem to understand? Does he seem interested? Does he ask intelligent questions? Does he seem able to put himself in the shoes of the potential reader of the book?

(d) Don't restrict yourself to talking business. Lead into some general conversation. Try to find out his hobbies and other spare-time activities. (Does he really have *time* to undertake a big job like a book?) Offer him coffee and a snack to make the interview relaxed and pleasant. Try, by every means possible, to size up his personality. A book collaboration is a long, close business, technical, and personal relationship. Do you think you can get along smoothly with this person for a couple of years or more, through a lot of hard work and, quite likely, some difficulties, delays, and exasperations?

(e) Remember all along that this interview is a process of *mutual inspection.* The writer is sizing you up, deciding whether *he* wants to work with *you.* So try to convince him that you really *are* an expert. This is no time for modesty; speak frankly of your abilities, achievements, and plans. Be prepared to whip out some press clippings, photographs, programs, prize certificates, etc.; these will deepen the impression you make. Remember, this is a *writer;* he tends to be impressed by written and printed material.

(f) If you decide that this candidate clearly would not suit your purpose, ease the conversation to a conclusion and let him go.

(g) With any candidate who makes a good impression, you can proceed to discuss financial terms. I suggest that a joint ownership of the copyright and a fifty-fifty split of the book's earnings is a fair arrangement. I would not take less than that.

There will be expenses in writing and selling the book. The writer should bear the costs of preparing the script and of postage in dealing with publishers. Costs of preparing illustrations may be shared by the two of you, on some ratio to be negotiated.

If there are prospects of earning money by lecturing, teaching, or broadcasting on the subject of the book, then all such earnings should go to the one who delivers the lecture, teaches the course, or does the broadcast.

(h) When you have chosen your collaborator and settled all the terms on which you intend to work, go to a lawyer or notary and have a contract drawn up.

## Caution!

You may meet a writer who urges you to pay him a fee for the writing, and then to put up all the cost of publishing the book yourself. I would advise you to be very cautious about any such proposal!

The commercial publisher's first task is to get a book edited, printed, and bound. (I have briefly described that process in Chapter 6.) Sure enough, you and a competent writer-collaborator could arrange for that editing, printing, and binding—at considerable cost, but without any overwhelming difficulty.

But the commercial publisher also has a nationwide—maybe international—organization for *publicizing*, *distributing*, and *selling* books. You have no such system. So, in a self-publication venture, you run the risk of finding yourself thousands of dollars out of pocket, with a basement full of books and no means of selling them!

The best way, for 99 percent of writers, is to deal with an established publisher, by the methods described elsewhere in this book.

## Planning

After you have chosen a writer-collaborator, you can get down to planning the book. Your objective statement should give the writer something to start with, but the two of you will need to spend considerable time in discussion.

I've covered the question of planning, for writers, in Chapter 4 of this book. Look over that chapter yourself; pay particular attention to these sections:

**Your Readership.**   Exactly who are you aiming at? You, with your specialized knowledge and experience of the subject, will have to take the lead in defining that readership. The writer will contribute something, too, from his knowledge of writing and publishing.

**Defining Your Subject.**   Beware the temptation to tell all you know; carefully choose the ground you will cover and cover it thoroughly.

**The Chapters.**   Think how your material may conveniently be divided into chapter-length sections. Decide in what order the chapters should be arranged. Create good chapter titles.

**Illustrations.**   How many, and of what kind, will the book need?
Make notes on these points and have them ready for the first working session with your collaborator.

**Revising the Draft.**   Consider carefully the hints that I gave to writers in that section. Realize that the preliminary plan is not going to be perfected on the strength of *one* interview. Painstaking, thorough work at this stage will improve your prospects of selling the script; moreover, it will ease the writing of the script after it has been sold.

## The Sample Section

See what I said in Chapter 5 under "Sample Section." To sell your book, you must provide a few thousand words of text, written in full. As you'll see from that chapter, you may not have full freedom in choosing what's to be offered as your sample.

Nevertheless, within such limits as are forced upon you, try to decide what you would particularly *like* to offer. The sample may be a good place to present some material you are especially proud of—something exclusive, something brand-new, something especially ingenious, beautiful, helpful, exciting—that will make your book stand out from whatever others the publisher may have seen lately.

Talk this over with the writer. Decide what you will choose for the sample. Then, between the two of you, prepare it, by interviewing, drafting, reviewing, and rewriting. Keep at the revision until both of you are fully satisfied with the sample.

## Selling the Book

The mechanics of selling—the typed script, the carbon copies or photocopies, the letters, the self-addressed stamped envelopes, etc.—can all be left to the writer. He should keep you informed of what's going on.

Selling may take a long time—at least a couple of months, maybe as much as several years. Maybe a publisher will suggest alterations to the plan, or the writing of an expanded sample section. Any such request should be regarded as a good sign; it means that the publisher is seriously interested in you and your work.

But, however long the sales process takes, don't sit brooding. Live your life, carry on with your specialty, much as you did before the idea of book writing entered your head.

One warning: Don't get yourself too tied down; don't make big, long-term working commitments that will leave you no spare time or energy for your book; don't fly off on a six-month vacation. You have already invested in this book project a lot of thought, time, and effort. You should hold yourself ready to cash in on that investment, and the opportunity to do so may come suddenly!

## After the Sale

A publisher accepts your proposal; you sign a contract, and bank, or spend, your cash advance. Now you *really* have to get down to work. There are several hundred pages of script plus, probably, a lot of illustrations to be produced under the pressure of a relentlessly approaching deadline.

The writer, if you have chosen a good one, knows how to organize the work. Cooperate with him. Faithfully keep interview appointments; carefully read script sections that he submits for your approval; produce, or find, necessary subjects for illustrations; deal tactfully with photographers and artists, if you are using them.

All this is exciting, but it's not a game! Keep reminding yourself that you are engaged in a major business transaction; you are investing a year or so of your life. So settle down and *work* at it; and demand that your collaborator do likewise.

## After the Writing

When the script and illustrations are packed up and mailed to the publisher, you can enjoy a little celebration. But you are still not free to go off on that six-month vacation! The publisher may ask for some alterations that he believes will make the book better and increase its sales. You would be wise to accept such a suggestion even though it involves another spell of hard, fast work.

Then, within the next few months, there will arrive two sets of proofs to be checked. The writer will do the technical work, but you should certainly inspect them as well.

Also bear in mind that you will be expected to help boost the sales of the finished book by various kinds of public activities—autographing copies in stores, interviews with press, radio, and TV, talks to interested organizations, and maybe other things, too.

Are you shy or inexperienced at facing the public? Then fill some of the waiting time between the end of writing and the publication day by taking courses in public speaking, acting, elocution, deportment, assertiveness training, or whatever you can find that might be useful. Such courses will not only help you promote the book, they will make you a more self-assured, happier person.

## Future Books

You are not forced to stop with one book. The publisher of your first book may suggest ideas for a sequel, or for a book on some allied subject. You may have some such book ideas of your own.

If you have worked well with the first writer, then you can ask him to collaborate with you again. If you did not get along well with him, then find another collaborator. You now know, better than before, how to make the choice.

Or, with this first collaborative book under your belt, you may decide that it's worth the trouble of becoming a writer yourself! I have seen this happen before; there's nothing to stop you from doing it!

## Summary

Your expertise: salable via collaborative writing.
Book collaboration: a long job, a big responsibility.
Preliminary steps:
    Analyze what's already published on your subject.
    Make notes for your own project.
The ideal collaborator: a successful nonfiction writer with how-to experience and with one or more books published.
There are lots of writers; just look for them.
Which one to use? A major decision, so choose with care.
Thoroughly discuss financial terms.
Draw up a contract for the project.
Beware of self-publication schemes.
Essential planning stages:
    Define your readership.
    Choose the right material.
    Divide it into chapters.
    Estimate illustration requirements.
    Keep revising till you are both satisfied.
Selling a book takes time; be patient.
After the sale, writing is a long process; persevere.
Finishing the script does not finish all the work.
Do your best to help promote sales.
Remember, you need not stop at one book.

# 8

# Working with an Expert- Collaborator

A lot of how-to books are produced by some form of collaborative effort. Undertaken wisely, and with luck, collaboration has advantages. You produce a book that, probably, you would never have written alone. With a good collaborator you find that two heads are, indeed, better than one. The work becomes exciting and highly productive, the two minds striking ideas off each other like flint and steel striking sparks.

Collaboration, if you find that it suits you, can be an important part, even the whole, of a satisfying, profitable writing career.

Yet collaboration has its risks, too. There are special technical problems in collaboration, which I shall describe later. There is the danger of severe clashes of personality. You may find that you have lost some freedom artistically, and are putting out writing that you know is less than your best. In most collaborative setups, you get only a part of the book's earnings.

## Choosing Collaborators

Choosing a collaborator for a book is a momentous decision. This is not like choosing a partner for a dance, or inviting an acquaintance to afternoon tea! You are going to work *closely* and *hard* with this person for six months, nine months, or a year. In other words, you are handing over a segment of your life to this person; you are investing a large chunk of your literary capital—skill, experience, and writing time; you are risking a part of your professional reputation on his reliability and honor.

Here are some points to consider before you commit yourself:

## Temperament

How will this person behave during the inevitable delays and minor crises on the path a book must follow from initial idea to finished script to published volume?

One author told me, "I collaborated with a woman who was very tense and jumpy from the start. She had a nervous breakdown in the middle of the project. She had probably never done any hard, systematic work before. When she recovered, she could work only very slowly. We had to ask the publisher twice for extensions of our deadline."

Some time ago, when I was younger and more careless, I made a deal, on December 11, to collaborate with a man on a subject of which I knew something and he knew a lot. On New Year's Eve he came charging into my home, drunk, accusing me of trying to steal all his knowledge and exploit it for myself! Luckily, this broke off the "collaboration" before any real work was done.

## Expertise

If you are planning a collaboration with an expert in some subject, be sure that he really *is* an expert.

If he is an artist or craftsman, check the quality and selling price of his work against other work on the market. Is he actively producing *now*? There will be disadvantages in working with someone who has retired and is out of touch with new developments in his subject.

Whatever the nature of his expertise, investigate his qualifications, degrees, awards, etc. What is his reputation among others in his field? (Beware of jealousy here!) Check the *scope* of his talents; if he specializes too narrowly, the proposed book may be impossible to sell.

## Accessibility

It is best if the collaborator lives close by, and is readily available; collaboration usually requires frequent meetings. Remember, your time and travel costs are part of your investment in the project!

I knew one instance where one of the collaborators was often away on business for two or three weeks at a time; that made the work slow and difficult.

## Business Sense

Can the proposed collaborator sincerely grasp the fact that you are going to engage in a big business deal that will take a year or more to show results in the form of a script? Results in the form of a printed book will probably take considerably longer than that. Financial returns, other than the publisher's advance, will take longer still.

Will he negotiate reasonably with you about the value of the contributions that both of you are going to make—technical knowledge, reputation, writing skill, time, script preparation, marketing ability?

Is he willing to sign a contract with you, even before any work is done on the book? Can he understand that contracts with you and, later on, with a publisher are legal commitments, to be fulfilled in every detail—wordage, illustrations, payments, deadlines, etc?

Is he going to be dependable in keeping appointments, checking drafts, reading proofs, and all the other unglamorous things that go into the making of a book?

Is he determined to produce the best book possible? Or is he going to press for some not-so-clever friend or relative to be used as illustrator or credited as coauthor and empowered to tamper with your writing?

Can he make a decision and stick to it? Or will he suddenly get the notion, a week before deadline, when the script and illustrations are ready for mailing, that he wants to have two or three chapters rewritten?

When the book comes out, will he do his share in the important business of promotion? Is he the shy, antisocial, noncommercial type who scorns advertising and yet expects the world to beat a path to his door? If he's a good speaker, friendly, outgoing, accustomed to radio, television, and live interviews, so much the better. If he has some means of pushing the sales of the book, say through courses that he teaches, stores that he owns, or other business connections, that's better still!

---

**Exercise 8:1**

Collaborator assessment score sheet. For each characteristic, score from 0 (quite unsuitable, useless, bad, etc.) to 10 (all one could desire). If the candidate scores 0 in any one category, or less than 20 total, you would do well to steer clear of him.

|  | Score |
| --- | --- |
| Temperament | _____ |
| Expertise | _____ |
| Accessibility | _____ |
| Business sense | _____ |

---

**Where Are They?**

There are three likely ways of finding collaborators:

1. They find you. For a magazine article, I interviewed a man who

ran a big business supplying materials and equipment to people who make wine at home. The interview was over; I stood up to go. The man pulled from a desk drawer a thick bundle of papers—some handwritten and some typescript. "I think I have the material for a book here," he said, "but I don't know how to write it. Would you be interested in collaborating with me?" Thus began my collaboration with Stanley Anderson, which eventually produced *The Art of Making Wine*, *The Art of Making Beer*, and *The Advanced Winemaker's Practical Guide*.

I suppose he had been impressed by my manner of conducting the interview. He proved to be the perfect how-to collaborator—a genuine expert, calm, businesslike in temperament, and only a short bus ride from my home.

So, by whatever means you can, show yourself, let yourself be known as a writer. Give people a chance to find you! (I shall have more to say about this in Chapter 15.)

2. You find them. Form the habit of sounding out the people you meet. Ask them what they do, what they know. In any case, it's a pleasant way to sustain conversation; most people like the chance to air their knowledge. Occasionally you will find someone who has the expertise that might make the basis for a collaborative book.

If you have a specific subject in mind, then go to places where you may reasonably expect to find experts—exhibitions and art galleries, craft stores and clubs, community colleges, night schools, universities. Look in magazines and papers that specialize in your desired subject; articles, photos, or advertisements may give you leads. Don't overlook the editorial staff—some of them may be experts, too. And remember your public library—librarians in the relevant divisions may have lists of people who are experts in subjects that you want.

3. A publisher or literary agent introduces you to someone who is looking for a collaborator. This could be a good bet, but all the same it's worth making your assessment of the candidate on the points mentioned earlier.

## Collaborative Contracts

You should have a written agreement with your collaborator before you undertake any significant amount of work. In such agreements, and in the publishers' contracts that will be signed when scripts are sold, a number of important issues must be decided.

### Credits

You, the writer, are collaborating with a technical expert who is a nonwriter. What form is best for the credits?

Normally the expert's name comes first. It is *his* subject; *he* is speaking, through you, to the readers.

How to Turn Dross into Gold

by

A.L. Chemist

So far, so good. Now, how is your name to be mentioned? On that point there may be room for discussion. It can be

A.L. Chemist and A. Scrivener

or

A.L. Chemist with A. Scrivener

Some writers feel there is a real, even an important difference between the two forms. The *and* (so goes the theory) would put the two collaborators on a more or less equal footing. *With* would imply that the writer is somewhat less important than the technical expert.

I doubt whether many *readers* would care about such a subtle distinction. Anyway, the book will certainly contain some introduction, foreword, or jacket notes fully describing the expert's technical and your literary qualifications.

A variation of this problem arises if you are both experts in the subject as well as writers. In this situation, there is no automatic rule as to whose name comes first. You must somehow decide it between you.

## Copyright and Royalties

If you are credited as joint author of the work, you should certainly be entitled to share the copyright and royalties. Fifty-fifty is the simplest sharing arrangement; I think a writer should ask for that at the start.

Some nonwriters may bridle at this. Then you must tactfully explain the expertise that you are bringing to the project. An expert may have spent years acquiring his skill, but you have spent years learning to write well enough to undertake a book.

Certainly in the writing of the book you will be doing far more work than the expert. Consider the typing alone. Show him the fees charged per day by commercial typing services. You will be typing several hundred pages of script *several times over* as the work moves through various drafts. If an expert tries to talk you down much below a 50 percent share, I would suggest that you think very carefully about whether you want to deal with him at all.

Remember that, in negotiating on copyright, you are concerned not only with the first edition and whatever it may earn. That copyright will cover later editions in other formats, revisions, and translations. For some subjects, film, videotape, or videocassette rights may be sold.

A successful how-to book can keep on earning money for decades.

So don't let yourself be bluffed or wheedled out of your fair share of that money.

### Other Earnings

Money earned by lectures on the subject of the book or other such personal appearances should go entirely to the person who delivers the lecture or makes the appearance. Bear in mind that such earnings may be very large. If you are a good speaker and your collaborator is not, you should do the lectures and set the fees.

### Cost of Illustrations

Illustrations for a how-to book can be quite expensive. I suggest that if you are publicly acknowledged as coauthor, it is appropriate for you to pay part of the cost of illustrations. Negotiate with the expert just how it is to be divided.

### Write It Down

Discuss with your collaborator these points and any others that specifically apply to your project. Then go to a lawyer or notary and get the agreement in proper legal form before you begin work.

## Planning the Book

Planning a collaborative book is likely to be a long, complicated task; it may call for considerable diplomacy on your part.

The technical expert who is not a writer may have little idea of what the structure of a good how-to book should be. His main idea may be simply to put on paper most of what he knows. He will press for the maximum number of illustrations to show what he has accomplished. He very likely sees the book as a form of self-glorification—something that he can brag about to fellow experts.

I do not condemn this objective; you should certainly aim to fulfill it. But you must, from the start, have other objectives in mind, too.

First, you as a writer want to plan and produce *a book that will sell*. Many nonwriters believe that any book-length mass of words, once typed on paper, will automatically be snapped up by a publisher! You may have to do some patient explaining of the way books are really sold, published, and distributed.

Second, you have a duty to your precisely defined group of readers to write a book that will be as useful to them as you can possibly make it. That may mean leaving out some things that would tickle the expert's vanity but would be of no interest, or of no use, to those readers.

Third, you have a duty to yourself. You are going to be coauthor, so you want to produce a book that is technically and artistically sound, that will enhance your reputation, too.

So in planning the book you should not be entirely swayed by what your collaborator wants. Indeed, before you have any detailed discussions with him about planning, do some research of your own.

## Check the Competition

You need to study carefully the existing books on the subject—some old, some new. For a start, your collaborator can probably lend you some. Take plenty of time to read them; make notes on subjects that will be useful to you in your planning.

(a) What things are covered in *all* the books?

(b) What things are included by some authors and omitted by others?

(c) What things seem to be the newest? What things seem to be obsolete, or on the way to obsolescence?

(d) Exactly where do the various books begin? How much do they assume that readers already know?

(e) In what order are various aspects of the subject treated?

(f) What illustrations do the various books provide? Photos? Diagrams? What seems most helpful? What seems unhelpful? Why?

(g) In this reading you will automatically familiarize yourself with the technical terms of the subject; you will be getting some general ideas about it.

Now you are ready to have a good talk with the expert. Discuss with him the questions mentioned above. Get his ideas on what is good and bad in the books he knows. Try to find out exactly what new, different material he has to offer. (You are making detailed notes all the time, of course.)

After this talk, do some more research on your own. Go to other experts—in libraries, craft stores, or wherever they may be found for your subject. Ask them what *they* think are the best books on the subject and *why*. If you have not yet seen those books, study them. Ask those other experts what is wrong with existing books in the field. You will probably get some valuable ideas from this criticism.

If there are any magazines dealing with your subject, read some recent issues of them. What are the articles about? Here you will find subjects and ideas that are up to date. Study the editorial pages. The editors are right on top of the subject; their jobs depend on understanding the interests and meeting the needs of their readers.

Study the correspondence columns. What do readers want to know? What are they pleased with? What are they angry about? These letter writers may be your potential readers. What kind of people are they? Try to size them up.

Study the advertisements. What products and services are being offered to the readers? At what prices? How much do these potential readers of your book seem willing to spend on their interest?

After all this research, you can go back to your expert and begin planning the book. You are still not as much an expert as he is, of course; but quite likely you know more than he does about some nontechnical aspects. You probably understand better than he does *what is being written* on the subject. (Though, of course, you won't tell him that in so many words.) Remember, an expert may build a fine reputation, may make a handsome living and keep working, working, working away on his own while drifting out of touch with the majority of people in his field.

**The Plan**

I described in Chapter 4 the main principles of book planning. Here are some special points you should consider in a collaborative project:

(a) Keep reminding yourself that this is a *how-to* book. The expert may want to include many descriptions and photographs of finished works, with inadequate instruction or no instruction on how the reader can make such things himself. You must tactfully oppose any such tendency.

(b) Occasionally an expert will want to put deliberate technical errors into a book! The purpose is to *stop* readers from producing the special effects or articles of which he feels especially proud. If you have acquired a fair technical knowledge of the subject, you should be able to detect and squelch any such tricks.

(c) What part of the subject should you use for the sample section? Careful thought on this can save you a lot of time and effort at this preliminary stage, when you are still working on speculation. Take something the expert has absolutely at his fingertips, something you can draw from him with a minimum of interviewing, that will need the least possible amount of independent research and checking. When drawing your plan, frame this aspect of the subject as a separate chapter or chapters.

**Revisions**

First, draft an outline and synopsis of the book. The outline should contain a summary of the expert's qualifications as well as your own. What does he know and what has he accomplished? Has he any formal qualifications—degrees, awards, honors, etc? Has he any experience in teaching the subject? Has he, either alone or in collaboration, written and published any other material on the subject?

Let your collaborator have your typed outline and synopsis for a day or two; then meet to discuss what revisions are needed. This time allowance for studying the draft is important! You will not get good results by simply handing him several thousand words and saying "What do you think of it?"

You will probably do three or four rewrites before both of you are satisfied. Meanwhile you can be drafting the sample section and starting to put that through the same inspection-consultation-rewriting procedure.

Take plenty of time over all this. Rushing and inadequate rewriting will result in an inferior proposal.

## Writing the Book

A collaborative book is sold in the same way as a solo work. But there are big differences in writing procedures.

### The Schedule

The publisher's contract is signed; the deadline is eight months or a year off. Your nonwriter collaborator is apt to think he's got more than enough time to take a vacation in Mexico (to spend the advance) and afterwards relax for a while and daydream about the fame and fortune the book will bring. You, the writer, must squelch any such ideas. There will be no time for vacationing or for daydreaming until the book is finished.

Heaven knows, there are enough possible delays and difficulties in the writing of a solo book. There are three or four times as many in a collaboration. Either partner may fall sick and be unable to work. Either partner's spouse or children may fall sick and stop her/him from working. Snow, floods, or other natural calamities may prevent the two of you from meeting. Strikes in postal or telephone services may stop you from communicating. There may be difficulties, misunderstandings, disputes, and delays with the person who is commissioned to make the illustrations. Moreover, you, the writer, will have several times more typing to do in a collaborative work than in a solo book.

News of the sale will produce a temporary flash of excitement for both of you. Take advantage of that to make a flying start with the work. Schedule regular meetings. For a start, try twice a week. That certainly should keep you both busy. Do all you can to make your partner fulfill the schedule. He may be unbusinesslike. He already has a reputation in his field and this book is only one extra item, perhaps not taken too seriously. But writing is your field; your reputation as a writer is on the line.

### The First Session

For your sample section you chose whatever was easiest and quickest to write. For actual work on the book, it is best to start at the beginning and work straight forward. Thus you can find, as early as possible, the manner of treatment and the degree of fullness that will properly cover the subject while giving you the right number of words.

(I know that in Chapter 7 I said there was no need to start at the beginning and work straight through. But *that* applies when you are working alone. In a collaboration it is so important and often so difficult to keep the nonwriter in a businesslike, productive frame of mind! The straight-through order of work helps to do that.)

For a typical how-to subject, the expert has tools, apparatus, materials, finished work, work in progress, samples, plans, records, etc., that you will need to examine and describe. And probably, with all his equipment at hand, he can most effectively *show* you what he means, as he explains technical points.

So consider the benefits of holding all, or most, of your work sessions at his home, workshop, studio, store, or office.

For Session 1, discuss whatever is going to be the first part of Chapter 1. Take notes or tape-record the conversation. If he already has made some notes, go over them together; get him to clarify or enlarge upon whatever needs such treatment.

In this and following interviews you have a dual function:

(a) You are the writer, getting material for the book.

(b) You are acting as *deputy for the reader*, that reader whose interests and requirements you now know very well. Keep on mentally asking "What would *the reader* want to know about this? Is there something here that the reader would not understand, would not believe?"

An expert, forgetting how he learned his subject, is likely to say "We don't need to explain that. *Everybody* knows *that.*" You, in your reader's deputy function, must prevent any such omissions. And you must keep the expert from going off on tangents. The work will be quite complicated enough if you proceed through it in order

## Rough Drafting

After Session 1 go home and, while the memory of it is fresh in your mind, write a rough draft of the material you have covered. Minor questions can be answered, minor gaps filled in, by phoning the expert.

Next day, revise the draft and make two copies of it, one for each of you. If your schedule and the efficiency of your postal service permit, mail the expert's copy to him. Otherwise, take it to him at your next interview. If you decide to do that, don't expect him to deliver a reasoned analysis of it at first sight. Leave it with him, and conduct the second interview like the first.

### Demonstrations

For many how-to subjects the expert will demonstrate to you various materials and techniques that you are writing about. Don't simply sit back and watch him. You will get much more from this aspect of the collaboration if you, as reader's deputy, actually try to do some of the things you are describing.

See what comes easily to you; feel what is most difficult. Find where the most detailed descriptions and instructions will be required. If it's practicable, take some materials home and experiment with them there. Throughout these demonstrations and personal experiments, keep on thinking, "Is there something here that is especially suitable for an illustration?"

### Regular Interview Format

Once you have begun regularly producing sections of rough draft, the interview format can be as follows:

(a) Look over the last section of rough draft. The expert has already had time to review it and think of changes he would like to see.

Discuss those changes. Many of them you will, no doubt, accept without question. But you probably have a much more accurate and detailed concept of the whole book than does the expert, so some of his proposals you may want to decline. "Yes, we will want to cover that; but I think it belongs in Chapter So-and-So, not here." (Promptly make a note of it to go in the Chapter So-and-So file.)

Or, "Yes, that's very good. But I think it's too difficult for this book. Perhaps we should save it for a sequel." (If you are already thinking of a sequel, you promptly make a note for that file.)

(b) Proceed to the next stage of interviewing and demonstrating.

### Chapter-by-Chapter

Keep rewriting your batches of rough draft along the lines agreed upon at your meetings. When you have a complete chapter in revised form, make a clean copy of it and let the expert check it.

He may have more revisions to suggest when he sees each chapter in complete form; the earlier you get them discussed and dealt with, the better. That is why the chapter-by-chapter procedure is more efficient and less worrisome than waiting till the whole script is in revised form before letting him see it.

### Two Writers

If you, as expert-writer, are collaborating with another expert-writer, some of the aforementioned procedures will not be necessary. Have a frank discussion before you begin the work and decide how to proceed. Some collaborators write alternate chapters of the book, then revise each other's first drafts. This procedure obviously calls for some tact. I have used this procedure, though that was for a biography, not for a how-to book.

## Illustrations

The general subject of how-to illustrations is covered in Chapter 13. There is one special point about illustrations for collaborative work. If you are hiring a photographer or artist to produce illustrations for the book, don't rely on your collaborator to oversee the work. You should personally supervise every photo session or every interview with the artist. Thus you make sure that the illustrations show exactly what the text of the book requires.

If the expert is himself an artist or photographer, don't just leave him to make the illustrations. You must keep on checking that he is doing the work promptly and properly, producing exactly the illustrations that are needed.

Some nonwriters do not understand the proper interaction of text and illustrations in good how-to writing. They tend to think that a lot of beautiful illustrations, so long as they are vaguely related to the subject, will make a handsome, serviceable book. Your supervision will ensure that you obtain the required illustrations of nuts, bolts, joints, stitches, undersides, insides, disassembled parts, and whatever else is going to be helpful to the reader.

## Ghostwriting

Suppose you collaborate with an expert who cannot write. He hires you to do all the writing for him, yet his name appears on the book. He takes all the credit, for both his knowledge and your authorship. This is *ghostwriting*.

There are sound reasons for someone being a ghostwriter. Maybe the ghostwriter, for good reason, prefers not to acknowledge publicly what he is doing. He may be an associate professor of literature who feels his colleagues would despise him if they knew. He may be a writer or editor with an exclusive contract to some newspaper, news service, magazine, or ad agency (i.e., he has promised not to write for anyone but his employer).

Also, some well-to-do ghost clients, hungry for the prestige of being "authors," pay very well indeed—far more than a writer could earn from doing the same amount of ordinary work.

Moreover, the value of the ghostwriter's fee may be markedly higher than the dollar figure suggests, if he can dodge paying income tax on it. (The client is not likely to blab about the transaction!)

There are several possible ways for ghostwriters to be paid.

## Flat Fee

The client pays you a flat fee out of his own pocket. Then,

(a) He may publish the book at his own expense, make his own arrangements to sell copies, and pocket the receipts.

(b) The book is sold in the usual way to a commercial publisher. Quite likely you will have to guide the client in this marketing, but he does it all in his own name and takes for himself whatever royalties the book may earn.

In either case, or in any similar situation, take these precautions:

## Time and Money

Carefully estimate, in advance, the amount of work that you will have to do. Maybe the expert has a substantial mass of typed notes or script containing all the needed material. A thorough editing will make it fit for publication.

Or maybe he has nothing on paper. He expects you to draw out of him, by persistent interviewing, all he knows and, if need be, supplement his knowledge by research. If that's the case, ask yourself some questions:

(a) Is he going to be a good interviewee? From your preliminary talks you can see whether he gives information quickly and coherently. If he is slow and hesitant, or if he is fast and scatterbrained, you will have to spend much more time with him.

(b) Is he going to be regularly available for interviews? Or will the calls of work, family, and pleasure often draw him away, and leave you twiddling your thumbs, unable to proceed?

(c) What will be your travel costs, in money and time, per interview? If extra research is needed, can he tell you exactly where and how to do it?

Consider these points and try to estimate how many months the work will take. I suggest emphasizing the word *months* in preliminary discussions with potential clients. Most nonwriters at first expect you to produce a book in a week or two!

Then decide how much per hour, or day, or month, you expect to earn. Maybe you have not previously thought of putting a dollars-and-cents value on your work. Then study the Help Wanted ads in your newspaper. See what is being offered for unskilled laboring work—pushing brooms, washing dishes, and such jobs. See the rates of pay for semiskilled and skilled tradespeople and for professionals. Where do you think you should be placed on that scale? You should also consider the expenses you would incur on the proposed book job. Then you can calculate the fee you should ask.

Here's another useful way to estimate. Check in a writers' directory the payment per word offered by a good how-to magazine that covers the same subject. That payment represents a fair reward for the skill of the writer plus a fair allowance for the time and expense of research. Multiply that rate by the wordage of the proposed book. See how well that estimate agrees with the results of your other calculation.

Too much trouble? Bear in mind that you are considering the sale of six, eight, ten, or twelve months of your life! It's not too much trouble to ensure that you are fairly paid for that irreplaceable commodity.

(I wish that someone had told me about this early in my writing career! How much waste in time, paper, backache, and eyesight I would have avoided; and how much heartbreak, too!)

Always bear in mind that people who hire ghostwriters are hungry for *glory*, for *prestige*! They should be, and can be, made to pay well for it.

---

### Exercise 8:2

1. Calculate working time for ghost-book.
    (a) Proposed wordage of book                          _____ words
    (b) Your average daily output of finished words including time spent on research, rewriting, etc.                          _____ words
    Estimated working time, a/b                          _____ days

2. Estimate fee.
    (a) Expected daily earnings                          $ _____
    (b) Estimated number of days                          _____
    Estimated fee, a times b                          $ _____

---

### Exercise 8:3

(a) Magazine payment per word for similar work          $ _____
(b) Proposed wordage of book                          _____
    Estimated fee, a times b                          $ _____

---

### The Contract

When the price is agreed on, get a written contract. Here are some important points to incorporate:

(a) Get an advance payment, about 20 to 25 percent of the total, before you begin work.

(b) More money should be paid, by proportionate installments, as the writing progresses.

(c) You will probably have to do the proofreading and indexing;

about 10 percent of the fee can be held back till you finish that.

However the details are arranged, the general principle must be that you never do any great amount of work on credit. That's to guard against the risk that the client might walk off with what you have written, and prove to be rich only in excuses for not paying!

The contract will also say that you make no claim to share the copyright of the work, to be known as the author of it, or to receive any payment for it, except what is specified in the contract.

Here is a rough draft:

### Agreement

It is agreed that A. Scrivener is to write for C. Lient a book, approximately x thousand words in length, provisionally entitled *The Art of Doing So-and-So*.

It is agreed that C. Lient will supply all information that A. Scrivener may require to complete the book.

The text and credits are to be framed so as to give C. Lient full and sole credit as author of the book.

If, for the preparation of illustrations for the book, it is necessary to engage artists or photographers, the costs of such work are to be borne entirely by C. Lient. Otherwise, the entire work and cost of preparing a script fit for submission to publishers shall be undertaken by A. Scrivener.

The responsibility of reading and correcting proofs and compiling an index shall be undertaken by A. Scrivener.

The copyright for the finished work is to be held solely by C. Lient; all royalties resulting from the sale of the book, or from the sale of subsidiary rights, are to go to C. Lient.

A. Scrivener guarantees that he will not use information gained during the preparation of this work to write any competitive work on the same or any allied subject.

[Alternative agreements for finding a publisher]

A. Scrivener shall undertake the work of seeking a publisher for the book; any expenses incurred in this work shall be borne by C. Lient.

[Or]

A. Scrivener shall be responsible only for writing a script fit for submission to publishers. The work and expense of finding a market for it shall be undertaken by C. Lient.

*Fees.* For completing the script, in form fit for submission to publishers, C. Lient will pay A. Scrivener the total sum of x thousand dollars. The manner of payment shall be as follows:

(a) On completion of this agreement, and before commencement of the work, _____ dollars.

    (b) On completion of _____ words, _____ dollars.
    (c) On completion of _____ words, _____ dollars.
    (d) On completion of _____ words, _____ dollars.
    (e) On completion of main text of the book, _____ dollars.
    (f) On completion of proofreading and indexing,
    _____ dollars.

From a draft like this, filled in with the appropriate figures, a lawyer or notary can draw a binding contract for the jurisdiction in which you live.

### Ethical Questions

Certain problems may arise in ghostwriting which would probably not be encountered elsewhere. How far do you feel responsible for the contents of the book, even though readers will never know you wrote it? What if some of the material your client wants to have you write is out of date or wrong? What if you recognize that some of it is dangerous or immoral?

Where does your responsibility to the client end and your responsibility to readers begin? For certain subjects you will have to think through these questions before signing any contracts.

### Royalties

Someone may ask you to ghostwrite for him and to take your pay in the form of a share, or all, of the royalties the book eventually earns. This is quite a gamble! Before you can even try to find a publisher you will need a serviceable book proposal consisting of outline, synopsis, and sample section. Especially if you are new to the subject, this will call for *a lot* of work—and you will be expected to do it with no guarantee of earning anything at all!

Of course, nonfiction authors do take that gamble all the time; but the risk seems more acceptable when you are working on *your own* chosen subject and for *your own* authorial credit!

I would advise against undertaking ghostwriting work under the royalty-sharing system.

## Not Good Enough

When you become known as a writer, you will quite likely receive offers such as "I will give you the idea for a book. You write it, and we split the proceeds fifty-fifty."

Such proposals should be rejected, politely or rudely as befits your temperament. No mere *idea* for a book is worth that much! Keep your antennae out, tuned in to your range of subjects; you will capture, free of charge, all the ideas you can use.

## Take Care

Does your collaborator already have some written drafts or notes at the start of the project? Good! That may save you some work. But be careful to check where the material came from. Did he really write it himself? Or did he copy it from someone else's book or magazine article? Tactfully explain to him the principles of copyright (see Chapter 11). Point out that copyright violations will injure his reputation, and may also hit him in the pocketbook.

Bear in mind, too, that one expert may use book writing as a means of attacking rival experts and criticizing their work. Watch for possibilities of libel. The line between legitimate criticism and malicious, damaging misrepresentation may not, in all cases, be well defined.

A libel suit by a disgruntled rival, even if it eventually fails, may be troublesome and expensive to both of you and to your publisher. Stirring up such a hornets' nest will injure your reputation.

So *be careful!*

## Summary

Collaboration: mixed benefits and difficulties.
Before choosing a collaborator, assess:
  Temperament
  Accessibility
  Business sense
Before starting work, get written agreement on:
  Credits
  Copyright and royalties
  Other earnings
  Cost of illustrations
Planning the book:
  Explain book writing and publishing.
  Check the competition.
  Do some independent research.
  Draft the outline and synopsis.
  For a sample selection, minimize the work.
Writing the book:
  Work to a schedule of interviewing, drafting, and revision.
  Work straight through, chapter by chapter.
  You are deputy for the reader.
Illustrations: personally supervise artists, photographers.
Ghostwriting: work, money, and anonymity.
  Negotiate a fair contract.
  Don't do much work without pay.
  Don't buy ideas at a high price.
Beware of copyright and libel problems.

# 9

# Local and Regional How-To Writing

Most writers (myself included) like to think of reaching, and moving, millions of readers with our words. We see ourselves signing contracts, shaking hands, facing TV cameras in New York, Tokyo, Paris, London, and so on.

That's all very well; a burning ambition does help to carry you through those early struggles. But don't let that ambition blind you to opportunities close to home!

Many books and booklets are written and published that will never have worldwide or nationwide distribution; they refer to subjects of special local or regional interest. By "local" I mean something that refers to a single site, to one town or city. "Regional" subjects refer to several neighboring towns or cities—maybe a whole state, or several adjoining states.

In the last month I have had two requests from local publishers for such books. The first would have been a how-to book for would-be speculators in mining stocks. The publisher believes that thousands of local people with money in the bank would like to dabble, or even take a deep plunge, into mining stocks—gold, silver, lead, zinc, copper, coal, etc.—but don't know how; and my hometown stock exchange is a noted center for that sort of investment.

This idea would interest precious few publishers in New York, Paris, or London; they all have their own investment facilities and opportunities. But *here* it *could* command interest—local mines, local stocks, local exchange, and local author.

Another publisher wanted an instruction book on spare-time gold prospecting. It's a popular hobby nowadays, he says; people are willing to spend lavishly on it. So he wants a book containing the basic technical information, plus details of regional mining laws and geology, and some regional maps. The proposed book would be sold not only through bookstores, but also through hardware and sporting-goods stores where the would-be prospectors go to buy tools, clothing, tents, stoves, maps, compasses, etc.

(It's not all fantasy. I heard three days ago of a local dentist, a persistent weekend and vacation prospector, who eventually made a rich strike and became a multimillionaire!)

New Yorkers and Parisians could not care less about my regional mining regulations or my hometown prospectors' outfitting places. But here, people do care; here, people will pay to get the relevant information clearly and concisely set down in a book.

I had to turn down those two propositions—I'm fully occupied in writing this book. But they fairly exemplify the kind of books that I'm writing about in this chapter.

## Local and Regional Opportunities

(From now on in this chapter, I am going to use the abbreviation *l-r* for "local or regional" and "local and regional.")

In my hometown bookstores and libraries I see scores of l-r how-to's on powerboating and sailing. They describe l-r waters, with l-r maps and photographs; they summarize averages and extremes of l-r weather; they list l-r boat building, boat launching, and boat repair facilities; they give directions to l-r fishing spots; they warn of l-r fishing laws and regulations. In short, they tell how to buy, operate, and enjoy boats under specific l-r conditions.

I see l-r books that concentrate on fishing, quite apart from boat ownership.

There is a successful how-to book on l-r scuba diving, well supplied with l-r charts of good diving spots, l-r figures of water temperatures, seasonal changes in underwater visibility, etc. No author in New York or Tokyo or Paris has that information; none of them would be interested in writing it, anyway. But here, it has been a bonanza for its publisher and author.

I see stacks of books about l-r legal problems: taxation; divorce; real estate purchases and sales; how to resolve landlord-tenant disputes; marriage contracts and separation agreements; how to incorporate private and public companies; how to make or probate a will; how to collect debts; how to understand and apply small-business laws and regulations; how to find tax shelters; how to fight traffic tickets; how to change your name. Some of the books emphasize how much the reader can do by himself, without a notary or lawyer. Others tell how, when using legal professionals, to save time and get best value for your fees.

Cookbooks emphasizing l-r ingredients, tastes, ethnic traditions, etc., sell well, not only to residents, but also to visitors and foreign tourists who want to take home something more than picture postcards.

## A Steady Demand

Ten years ago, the only l-r books published around here were a few histories and tourist guides. Now there's this flood of how-to books, a flood which shows no sign of subsiding.

A city 150 miles from here is served by a brilliantly successful shoppers' guidebook. It lists every retail store in the city and suburbs, and tells briefly what each one sells and what services it offers. By a suitable system of indexing and arrangement, it shows the potential purchaser how to find *anything* he wants to buy, and advises on how to make the best possible deals for cash, credit, or barter. (Obviously, this information can be useful even for longtime residents, but it is especially valuable to newcomers who, in that part of the country, number in the tens of thousands per annum.)

This book is updated every second year, so it provides a long-continuing source of revenue for its publisher and author.

## An Uncertain Supply

Two years ago a local publisher planned to bring out the same sort of book here in my hometown, but he could not get anyone to write it! Three writers tried, but they all wanted to do it *their* way—not the well-proven way that the publisher wanted, the way that he knew would sell.

I am writing this page on December 30th. On the 27th I had breakfast with the same publisher, and he gave me a year-end review of his operations. He had planned to publish six new l-r books this year, three of them in the how-to category. Three of the six authors failed to deliver their scripts at all; the other three submitted scripts so bad that the publisher had to send them back for major rewriting. The result: *no* new l-r books this year!

Why do writers act like this? OK, if you're writing poetry, by all means do it your own way. But if you want to write how-to books, then prepare yourself to take direction from publishers. This applies especially to someone attempting a *first* how-to book! And be reliable! Deliver *what* you promised, *when* you promised it! (I hope that, by harping on these ideas, I can get some readers to accept them.)

**Exercise 9:1**

Compile a list of l-r how-to books published in your area within the last five years.

1. Analyze *how strong* is the l-r connection: how many, if any, of those books could just as easily have been researched, written, and published in New York, London, Ottawa, or elsewhere? Score from 0 = no particular l-r connection, to 10 = an exclusively l-r connection.

2. List the books by publishers; see if you can discover the policy of each publisher on such points as:

(a) Subject

(b) Length

(c) Style

(d) Illustration

(e) Binding

(f) Price

(g) New editions or revisions

(h) Collaborations, i.e., does he seem to shy away from them, or does he regularly use them?

## Think like a Publisher

If this kind of writing interests you, don't sit back waiting for l-r publishers to come knocking at your door.

Study l-r newspapers and magazines. You will see the occasional statement that "The public needs to know more about this . . ." You will read stories of people who got into legal, emotional, health, or some other kind of difficulties because they did not know how to do this, that, or the other.

Talk to l-r people—friends and strangers. Try to find out what they would like to do, if only they knew how: how to run in l-r elections; how to organize a l-r country fair; how to set up a restaurant; how to manage household finances under l-r economic conditions, etc.

Through this scouting procedure, force yourself—at least part of the time—outside of your writer's personality. The typical writer's line of thought is, "What would be the most enjoyable for me to write, and make me the most money for the least work?" (I'm not condemning that line of thought! It's natural; we all follow it.)

But try to see also the publisher's point of view: "What would give me the least trouble and expense in production? What would have the widest possible appeal to l-r readers? What would be easy to publicize via l-r print, broadcast, and other media? What would be the most suitable addition to my present list, and make me the most money?"

Don't skimp on the scouting! Don't expect to get it all done in one

week or one month. You're making yourself *an expert* in this re-
stricted field, where the competition is very slight, and where you
are planning to become a star performer.

---

**Exercise 9:2**

Make a short list of potential l-r how-to titles. Open a file for each
idea as soon as you get it, and begin gathering clippings, notes, etc.
(Detailed instructions for this procedure appear under "The Production Line" in Chapter 15.)

---

# The Direct Approach

In this l-r field you can, if you wish, vary the procedures for approaching publishers that I described earlier in the book. Here, personal contact may, under certain conditions, be the quickest, most
effective, and most enjoyable means to start the ball rolling. Here's
the strategy I would recommend.

(a) Pick out two or three how-to book ideas that would appeal to
one publisher. If there are several l-r publishers, then maybe, from
studying the books that they put out, from gossip with other writers,
or other sources, you can decide which one you would prefer to
work with.

(b) Taking plenty of time, make a really slick, professional-look-
ing outline for each book. Rewrite, rewrite, rewrite, always keeping
in mind the publisher's point of view. Get it down to about 350
words and type a perfect copy. Also type a perfect title sheet and clip
it to the outline. (If you have only one idea to offer, then prepare the
title sheet and outline for that alone.)

(c) Phone the publisher and say, "I have a couple of book proposals that I'd like to put to you." But don't beg for a chance to see
him at his office. Invite him out to lunch! This will almost certainly
make a good impression. Offer him a choice of two dates in the very
near future; ask what time is convenient for him; then tell him to
meet you at such-and-such restaurant.

Carefully plan a few words of self-description so that he can instantly recognize you; add some special detail such as "I'll be carrying a brown briefcase," or "I'll be wearing a red raincoat."

(d) The plan of the lunch is based upon some words of wisdom
written by the Earl of Chesterfield (1694-1773) to his son: "Whenever you meet with a man eminent in any way, feed him, and feed
upon him, at the same time."

Accordingly, you will not only make your presentation to the publisher, you will also try to *learn* from him as much as you can. Keep
that point in mind throughout!

(e) You meet at the rendezvous, identify yourself, get seated, and buy him a drink for a start. Don't plunge into your own business right away. Begin with some pleasant conversation about *him* and his affairs.

Be prepared with some remarks about one of his recent books—a successful one. Ask some intelligent questions about it. For example: did he come up with the idea for the book himself? Or was it submitted by the author? How long did it take from inception of the idea to publication? Were there any special difficulties with the publication of that book? If there are particularly good illustrations, maps, etc., let your compliments and questions cover those as well as the text.

Ask him what is his biggest single problem with authors.

If he comes out with a whole catalog of complaints about authors (as is quite likely), don't argue; don't rush to the defense of the tribe of writers! Listen! Learn! Keep asking supplementary questions; lead him on to talk freely. Try your hardest to remember the main points; but at this stage don't take notes.

Then, at some convenient time, after the main eating is over, lead on to the ideas you want to present. The best way is to hand him two of your outlines together; or, if you have only one, hand him that. (Don't show him three at once—that's too much of a good thing.)

While he glances through the outlines, whip out your pen and paper, ready to note down his comments. Ask him which of the two he prefers. Offer to send a detailed synopsis of that one in a few days.

If he likes neither, bring out your third item and show it to him. If he likes that, similarly offer a detailed synopsis.

If he does not like the third one either, then ask him if he has any ideas of his own that he's seeking a writer for. Take careful note of what he says. If he comes up with any idea that is within your scope of interest and writing ability, then offer to draw up an outline for it. (That should not be too hard, if you lead him on to say all he knows and thinks about the subject.)

If he has no such ideas awaiting action, you end up with a twofold suggestion:

1. Offer to submit more ideas to him later on, when you can come up with them.

2. Ask him to keep you in mind when he needs some writing done.

This approach is absolutely different from that made by most writers! It will make the publisher remember you as someone quite outstanding.

Remember, by an interview like this you have gained *precious information*, well worth the cost of the lunch even if you don't immediately make a sale! For many writers, the cost of the lunch and tip will be a tax-deductible expense, so make sure you get a receipt.

### Objection Overruled

"Wait a minute, Hull!" someone protests. "This all sounds phony—hypocritical. *Planning* an interview! Using tactics! Not saying exactly what you think, when you think it!"

I suggest rather that such an interview is a legitimate way of presenting yourself as the kind of writer that a publisher would like to deal with.

The chance to do this is one advantage you gain by venturing into the l-r market; you cannot do it so well if you are working at the national or international level.

---

### Exercise 9:3

Begin a detailed, written plan for your direct-approach interview. Draw up the outline(s). Select the publisher and the restaurant. Plan your opening remarks.

---

## An Alternative

If for some reason—insuperable shyness on your part, or the publisher's refusal to meet you—the aforementioned scheme is impracticable, then use the straightforward proposal-by-mail system described in Chapter 5. Even with this method, a really slick, high-quality proposal will set you apart from the majority of l-r authors.

But anyway, in this near-to-home market you will, sooner or later, have to be prepared for face-to-face interviews with publishers or members of their staffs.

## Product Instruction Books

Some atrocious writing is being foisted on the public in the shape of product instruction books. I remember when I bought my first slide rule, the booklet that came with it was so inadequate and so riddled with errors that I could not use the rule! I had to go out and buy a book on slide rule operation. Precisely the same thing happened with my first hand-held electronic calculator.

I have before me a recent newspaper review of the instruction book for a new computer program. The review complains about typographical errors, so that practice computations do not give the answers shown in the text; no instructions on how a chosen program can be edited or reviewed; sections that are nearly unintelligible, even to the mathematician who wrote the review.

I assume that such inadequate instruction manuals are written by engineers, machinists, salesmen, accountants, or some other employees of the manufacturers. What the customers need are manuals written *by writers*.

### Your Prospects

Who, in your area, is making products that need instruction books? Are some of the existing books in need of improvement? Could you do it?

Do some research, as if you were going to write an article on "Instruction Books." Find out what readers of the books think of what they are getting. What more would they want? Find out what retailers of the product think; they are probably aware of how their customers react to poor instruction material.

Make a detailed analysis of some defective book; write politely to the manufacturer and ask for an interview. Present your ideas for a better instruction book. Even if they won't reprint the present book or books, ask them to let you have a try at writing any new ones they need.

For any such job you undertake, get a written agreement stating what you are going to do and how much you are to be paid. For such work, the royalty system is inappropriate, as there is no retail selling of the printed book. So a lump-sum payment is probably the best.

How much to ask? That depends on how long the job will take, and on how much you figure your time is worth. The beginner, in this or any other field of activity, should not expect to drive too hard a bargain. So, for a start, don't hold out for such big fees that you never get any jobs!

Remember, *you are learning as you write*. Moreover, the reward of the first few jobs in the field comes, not only in cash, but also from their effect in establishing your reputation. When you have several successes to your credit, you can command higher prices.

Whatever fee is agreed on, ask for a fair proportion—say one-third or one-half—in advance, and the rest on completion.

## Advertise

If you can't make direct contact with potential customers, you can advertise in l-r papers. Try something along these lines in the "Professional Services" classification of a daily or weekly newspaper:

Inventors, craftsmen, manufacturers! Writer will do articles, technical and business; how-to manuals, product instruction leaflets or books; ads or love letters. Call So-and-So, Phone No.

_____

Get some cards printed, with wording similar to the ad, and distribute them where you think they may do some good.

Undignified? Inartistic? Perhaps. But we how-to writers want to make money—and it pays to advertise!

## Summary

L-r markets are large, and competition is not strong.
Try to think like a publisher, some of the time.
For a l-r publisher, try the direct approach.
Product instruction books need writers.
Advertise yourself in the l-r market.

# 10

# Working Methods: How to Ease the Job — A Little

When you sit down to write you may find, as many others have found, that your knowledge of the subject is deeply buried. You know it's there, but it is not in the form that you now need.

You may have a keen eye for what is "right" or "wrong," for what is "good," "so-so," or "bad" in your art, craft, or business. You may have exquisite muscular skills for cutting, shaping, and joining. Yet perhaps you have never had occasion to haul these abilities, these tastes, to the surface of your mind and express them on paper.

The unearthing of what has been unconscious, the putting into words of what has been nonverbal, the communication of what has been personal—these are the basic processes of how-to writing.

## Making Notes

Here is one step you can take, right from the moment you decide to write about your subject. You need not wait till you have defined your readership, drafted your proposal, found your publisher, or anything else. It is never too soon to start making notes!

### Watch Yourself

At any convenient time when you are doing practical work on your subject, *make notes*. If you can, write or type the notes when you take a break from whatever you are doing. If that's awkward, you can speak into a tape recorder while you are working. If you do that, be sure to transcribe the material as soon as possible. You want the experience of putting it *on paper*, and notes on paper are twenty times quicker and easier for reference than the same material on tape.

Now, what sorts of things should go in those notes?

**Mention materials and equipment.** Give full details. For example, if there is any choice in the matter, tell what grade of a certain material you would recommend and why. Tell where to get it, how much of it to buy at a time, and, if necessary, how to store it. What if the preferred material or grade is not available? What can be substituted?

Can you offer any general hints on how to save money in buying? For a magazine article, it may be useful to mention specific costs per ounce, per yard, per liter, etc. But for a book, price changes are likely to make such figures out of date before they ever see print. Moreover, your book will—you hope—have a long sales life; that would further outdate those prices.

If you have time, it may be worthwhile to briefly note the history of some old materials (e.g., in the textile arts, wool, cotton, and silk), the development of substitutes (e.g., synthetic fibers), and maybe a brief prediction of future inventions and discoveries.

For equipment, in magazine writing you can quote dollar prices, but for books, avoid them. You can always cite *relative* costs of various types, if you have them at your fingertips.

---

**Exercise 10:1**

Make at least a page of notes on materials and equipment for your subject.

---

**Describe desirable working conditions.** Should the reader stand or sit? What size workbench or table do you use or recommend? (Many people muddle along in working conditions far inferior to those they know are best!) Have you developed any little tricks to make the work easier and more efficient?

For instance, I find that store-bought desks are too low for me; they give me a pain in the shoulders and neck. So I put a 1-inch (25-mm) block of wood under each leg of the desk; that lets me write in comfort.

By contrast, store-bought typewriter tables are too high for me; they tire my arms. So I broke the casters off mine, which brought it down to a comfortable level.

**Exercise 10:2**

Make at least a page of notes on working conditions for your subject.

---

**Describe, step by step, what you are doing.** Describe it in full detail. Observe yourself in action and record what you see and feel and hear. What is your left hand doing? What is your right hand doing? How far are your eyes from the work? How many strokes a minute are you making? Just how long did each stage of the procedure take?

For example, at this moment I am sitting at my raised-up desk, 30.5 inches (77 cm) high. (By the way, because I often need such figures in my work, I keep a slide rule metric converter close at hand to provide them quickly.)

I have already typed a draft of this chapter through paragraph (c). I am writing this paragraph with a ballpoint pen.

On a sheet next to me I have handwritten drafts of the first two exercises for this chapter. My usual method is to work through the main text of a chapter first, and then insert the exercises where they seem to fit best. This avoids the difficulty of trying to make several decisions at once.

On another sheet I am composing a handwritten draft of the summary for this chapter as I go along.

The writing from "For example," above, down to this line has taken thirty-five minutes.

Think of some other experts you know in your subject area. How do they work? Do they have any procedures noticeably different from yours? Could some of those alternative procedures be worth describing in the book?

---

**Exercise 10:3**

Make at least a page of notes on working methods for your subject.

---

**Note particularly the difficult spots, where things are likely to go wrong.** What did you do this time to prevent those mistakes or failures? Have you heard from fellow experts of any other methods they use to overcome such difficulties?

One writer told me he always stops work in the middle of a sentence. Next morning he will find little difficulty in completing that sentence, so he overcomes the psychological problem of getting started!

Note, also, anything that did actually go wrong and what you did to correct it. This sort of material will be especially valuable to your readers.

**Exercise 10:4**

Make at least a page of notes on some difficulties likely to be encountered by your readers; give your favored methods of overcoming them.

---

**Another good way to get ideas is to review some of your past successes.** If your subject involves making things, you may have a table, a vase, a set of chessmen, etc., or a photograph of the finished article. With intangibles—directing a play, making a speech, conquering some bad habit—you have your memories. So draw on your memory and make notes of what you find.

You will find it easier to start writing notes on "how I made one particular vase" than on "general techniques of vase making."

### The Value of Notes

Make all the notes you can! This note making opens up the thought channels in your mind that will be used for the actual writing. Note making done along the lines I have suggested will create for you a rich stock of practical examples, many of which will serve to illustrate points that you want to make in the text of the book.

Many of the notes may be rough—no sentence structure, no grammar—just enough to remind you of a fact or an idea that will be useful in the writing.

Here, for example, is one of my notes for this chapter: "Explain 'turning away' creativity phenom." You will see later on what developed from those few words.

Sometimes you may find that you can quickly note down a paragraph, two paragraphs, even a page, in coherent, correct, more or less finished form. That's exciting. Enjoy it when it happens, but don't strain for it, and don't feel guilty when you don't achieve it.

Always bear in mind that the notes are not your script but the *raw material* from which you will make a script or scripts. The more abundant the supply of raw material, the more discriminating you can be in selecting from it, and the easier will be your work.

So be persistent and enthusiastic in your note making. With fat files of notes, you will find it much easier to begin drafting the script.

## Chapter Files

As soon as you have anything on paper concerning a chapter—just one sheet with the chapter title, a rough draft of the chapter summary, some research notes, some newspaper clippings, a list of required illustrations, some rough sketches for diagrams, or what-ever—open a separate file for that chapter. If you want to be fancy about it, you can use a manila file folder for each chapter. I usually improvise chapter files from big envelopes cut open or from folded ₰ ₁eets of paper; I save the manila folders for correspondence, contracts, final drafts, and such things.

Whatever the physical arrangement may be, the important thing is to devise some system. Then, whenever you find some new piece of material or get some new idea that may refer to a particular chapter, you can pick up that chapter file; instantly you have in hand everything, used and unused, concerning that chapter.

**Exercise 10:5**

Open a full set of chapter files for your book.

# First Drafts

I said in Chapter 4 that you need not wait for final revision of a book outline before starting on the chapter plan. That principle applies to other stages of your work: it's worth a little more explanation.

Writing an article or a book is a complex job. There are many parts to be combined into a whole—something like building a house. As with the house, some parts need a lot of preliminary processing even before they are brought to the site; on site they may need more adjustment—cutting, hammering, bending, and so on—before they will fit into place. And, when in place, they require various finishing processes—sanding, priming, painting, and such—before they begin to serve their function.

Don't expect to proceed smoothly through the article, or chapter, or book, getting each sentence and paragraph perfect as you go. Be satisfied to set each piece of material down in rough form at first.

Perhaps, for the moment, that rough draft is the best you can do. You may feel there's something wrong with it but not see how you can make it better. Don't sit scratching your head and worrying! Lay that piece aside and work at something else.

Even as you write your first draft you may get ideas for rewriting it. I would suggest that, if the first-drafting process is going smoothly, you *drive ahead with it*. Don't keep stopping to rewrite. But have a separate sheet handy and briefly note down those rewrite ideas so that they will be ready when you want to use them.

Recognize that first drafts are likely to be rough. Don't strain for exact words at this stage. Use the nearest word you can think of or even leave a gap to be filled in later. Pound away; get the first draft down somehow, *anyhow*.

**Exercise 10:6**

Write one page of first draft; no matter how rough it is, get one page finished.

## Points of Attack

In writing a nonfiction book, there is no particular reason to begin at the start of Chapter 1 and work through in order—Chapters 2, 3, 4, etc.—right on to the end. There is no reason why you have to continue this morning where you left off yesterday.

From your plan you know the elements or "units" which go to build up each chapter.

What I am calling a "unit" is the part of a chapter marked off by a subhead. This part under the subhead "Points of Attack" is one unit. A long unit may be built up of several subunits, marked by sub-sub-heads. For example, the unit in this chapter on "The Two Faculties" has two subunits.

A notable advantage of this unit system is that it gives you many "points of attack" on your project. You may find yourself bogged down at one place, perhaps because some piece of information is not yet in hand, perhaps because you simply can't think what to write next. Don't sit there struggling, worrying! Turn to another unit of the book where you can go ahead rapidly, easily.

For example, yesterday I wrote five pages of the "Interviewing" unit in Chapter 11, then all of the "Literary Agents" unit in Chapter 15. Now I am writing this unit of Chapter 10.

## Page Numbering

In the final clean copy of a book script the pages should be numbered consecutively from beginning to end. But that numbering system would be impractical during the early and middle stages of writing the book. The system I recommend makes use of a simple code based on chapter numbers and unit titles.

For example, in my first draft I put the number 10 at the top right-hand corner of the sheet because this is part of Chapter 10. Then I put the letters pn (representing the unit title, Page Numbering), a colon, and the digit 1.

The full code sign is thus 10 pn:1. That designation will serve through however many rewrites are needed.

Similarly, for the "Two Faculties" unit, later in this chapter, the sheets are coded 10 tf:1, 10 tf:2, 10 tf:3, etc.

Hold the sheets of each unit together with a paper clip. Store all the units of each chapter in the appropriate chapter file.

During the rewriting process there are going to be insertions, cancellations, and transfers of pages; maybe whole units will be switched from their original chapters to others where you feel they fit more appropriately. This coded page numbering system will facilitate such changes. It will also be useful when you are writing notes to yourself—directions to check, to refer to, or to coordinate with something in another part of the book.

**Exercise 10:7**

Install this page numbering system on whatever material you have drafted so far. Keep it up to date as you proceed.

## Chapter Wordage

After you have estimated the total length of your book, you can break down that total to allot an approximate wordage to each chapter. From your knowledge of the subject you realize that some chapter subjects are more complex and more important than others. Those complex, important subjects will demand longer chapters than will the simpler ones.

**Exercise 10:8**

Make a list of chapters. Give to each a provisional wordage so that all the chapter totals add up to the book total that you determined in Exercise 4:12.

## Controlling Wordage

If you are writing a 1,500-word article, you have little difficulty in controlling the length of it. You know that the finished script must be about six pages of pica type, or five of elite. So you can see at a glance whether your early drafts are too short or too long.

With a 75,000-word book it's not so simple. You have several hundred sheets of paper, some full of typing, some partly blank, some containing many deletions, some with part-sheets stapled on to hold extra material.

It is annoying to think you have finished your book and then find that you are 10,000 or 15,000 words short of your contracted total. Even if you sent in that script, the publisher would make you write enough extra text to bring it up to the proper length.

On the other hand, it's a waste of effort to write twice as much as you need and then have to make huge cuts for your final draft.

I know that, earlier in this chapter, I said, "Make all the notes you can." But there is no great mental effort in making *notes*. They are scraps of information obtained from various sources; they are random ideas about your project that have popped into consciousness by themselves. They are your raw material, so by all means have plenty of that raw material.

But the first draft requires hard, prolonged mental and physical work! Why make the work any harder, any longer than necessary? Here is a simple way to keep control of wordage, from the first page right through to the end.

1. At the bottom of each page pencil in the number of lines it contains. I recommend using a pencil to allow easy correction of the total when you make cuts or additions to the page in the course of rewriting. A part-line, as at the end of a paragraph, counts as a whole line. A title, subhead, or sub-subhead counts as a line, too; it will occupy a whole line in the printed book.

2. When you complete the draft of one unit, add up its total linage. Pencil that in at the top of the first page of the unit. Multiply that figure by ten for pica type, or by twelve for elite, to get a useful approximation of the unit wordage.

3. On the front of the chapter file, write the names of the units it contains; pencil in the wordage of each.

4. At the bottom of the file cover, keep a penciled total of the words written to date in that chapter.

5. On a separate list of chapter subjects, keep an up-to-date list of word totals. This shows you exactly how much you have written and how much you have to write. It also lets you check that you are keeping the proper balance of length between the chapters (I discussed that under "Chapter Wordage" earlier). Be sure to guard against big, unjustified departures from that planned balance.

Here is an example of how the system works. This is what the front cover of this chapter file contains as I draft this page.

Chapter 10
Working Methods

| | |
|---|---:|
| Intro | 170 |
| Making Notes | 1,460 |
| First Drafts | 390 |
| Points of Attack | 300 |
| Page Numbering | 300 |
| | |
| Total to date | 2,620 |

(That does not include the wordage of this unit, which is not yet finished; and there are more units still to come. So the eventual chapter wordage will be greater. The point is that I know exactly where I stand *now*.)

**Exercise 10:9**

Install this wordage control system on whatever material you have drafted so far. Keep it up to date as you proceed.

# Rewriting

In any kind of writing—for books, magazines, the stage, radio, television, etc.—you will have to do some rewriting. Indeed, some writers say that the business consists of 10 percent writing and 90 percent rewriting.

Here are some hints to make rewriting faster and easier:

(a) Form the habit of *rapid* rewriting. Do it piecemeal, not all at once. Work fast, each time around, correcting the faults you can see. Don't brood on it; don't feel that the second draft has to be perfect. Make whatever improvements you can on the unit or chapter that you have before you; then put it away for a while and get on with something else.

An advantage of the delay is that it lets you come back to the script with a sense of unfamiliarity. You obtain to some extent the view of a reader seeing it for the first time. That is the view you need for effective rewriting.

Five fast rewrites take less time and less effort than two laborious ones; and they produce a better result.

(b) If you did not have the wordage right on your first draft, make a point of getting it right, or very close to right, on the second draft. There's no point in spending thought, time, and physical effort in polishing a script that is far from the right length.

(c) A lot of the rewriting can be done with pen and ink—crossing out words and lines, writing in better material, transposing paragraphs, etc.

(d) Keep thinking about the questions of order. Are the units of each chapter in the best possible order for a reader coming fresh to the subject?

(e) Here's a trick to use if you sit down for a session of rewriting but can't seem to get started. Take a page that has a lot of handwritten alterations and make a clean typed copy of it. In the typing you will probably be able to make a few more small improvements. Even if that's not so, the typing will get your brain into gear for the work that is to follow.

(f) Another trick I use is to leave fifty or sixty words in handwriting at the end of one day's work. Revising those few lines and typing them out is an easy way to get going the next morning.

(g) When preparing to rewrite a chapter, you'll find it helpful to lay out the separate units in a row on your desk or on a table.

Thoughtfully scan the unit titles; look over the opening paragraphs of the units. Ask yourself, "Are these precisely the components that I need to fulfill the purpose of this chapter?"

Spend a few minutes thinking—easily, pleasantly. This procedure makes it easier to check for gaps that need to be filled in. Similarly, you can check for possible rearrangements of the material. The "unit" system that I described earlier in this chapter makes such rearrangements quick and easy. Entire units can be moved around like building blocks.

For example, on my second rewrite of Chapter 4, I found that I had two separate references to the need for precise definition of the subject. Neither of them was complete in itself. I decided that the most effective treatment would be to combine those two items under one subhead. I did that, and produced the unit entitled "Defining Your Subject."

---

**Exercise 10:10**

Use these procedures to do a rapid rewrite of a chapter or some substantial piece of material that you have drafted.

---

# Indexing

A how-to book is not going to be read straight through like a novel and then laid aside. It is going to be looked at frequently—a formula here, a diagram there—as the owner, the student of whatever you are teaching, seeks various bits of information. For such reference, the reader will probably want to consult an index.

Moreover, librarians usually prefer an indexed book to one with no index; they realize that the index makes the book more valuable for reference. (Bear in mind that sales to libraries may be an important factor in a book's success!)

The contract for a nonfiction book customarily requires that the author make the index. (He is supposed to have the best knowledge of the book's contents.) Often a part of the advance payment will be held back until the index is completed.

Making the index—if indexing is required—will be the last thing you do for your book before surrendering it to the publisher, the printers, the bookstores, and the public. But, for various reasons, you should begin thinking about and working on the index almost from the start. That's why I raise the subject in this chapter.

### Preparation

Obviously, an index cannot be *finished* till you have the numbered proof pages before you. And, if your book proceeds like most books, the page proof checking will have to be done in haste. If, at the same time, you have to do the whole indexing process, you'll be likely to make mistakes. To avoid that hurry and stress, you can get most of the indexing work done ahead of time. Here's how:

(a) While writing the book, bear in mind the typical reader who will be using it. Keep asking, "What would the reader want to refer to in this part of the book?"

Also ask yourself, "How can this or that item be referred to most effectively, most concisely in the index?"

(b) Get a few hundred index cards, 3x5 inches (7½x13 cm). As you come up with each potential index item, write it on a card. Also put on the card the script page number or numbers relevant to the item. For early drafts use the page number code that I described earlier in this chapter. Keep the cards in alphabetical order.

After you send off the clean copy of your script to the publisher, go through your index cards again and substitute the final script page numbers. That gives you something constructive to do while you are waiting for the galley proofs.

## Completion

When you eventually get the page proofs, most of your indexing work will already be done. You'll have only to substitute the printed page numbers for the script page numbers. That should not take long. Then make a clean copy of the whole index on regular-sized sheets.

# Contracting Out

Are you, perhaps, one of those writers who find the thought of proofreading or indexing their own books absolutely repugnant? There are, in most cities, skilled people who will do these punctilious jobs for a fee. But don't wait till the arrival of the proofs to start searching.

Look in the Yellow Pages of your phone directory, under "Editorial Services," "Secretarial Services," "Stenographers—Public," "Writers," and such headings. Ask at your public library, in the Language and Literature departments, if they know anyone who does freelance editing and indexing. Find out who runs the book review section of your newspaper; ask him the same question.

Find your substitute proofreader and indexer, make your deal well in advance, and be ready with the money for his fee.

Many publishers will take care of finding and contracting with an indexer, deducting the indexer's fee from your royalties.

# The Two Faculties

The human mind, so far as a writer is concerned, is divided into two sections, or faculties: the rational and the creative. The rational faculty sets problems; the creative provides solutions. The rational faculty discovers facts; the creative faculty produces ideas. The production of solutions and ideas is often sudden and unexpected; it is what poets and mystics have called "inspiration"; but we nonfiction writers can cultivate it and use it for our work, too.

My first awareness of this process came one day when I was doing a difficult crossword puzzle. I solved about two-thirds of it and then got absolutely stuck. I thought and thought in vain. I gave up, laid the puzzle down, made myself a cup of coffee and drank it slowly, looking out the window, idly watching the ships go by.

Then I picked up the puzzle again, intending to throw it away. But suddenly I saw the answer to one clue that had baffled me before! I filled it in. Then, one after another—click, click, click—came all the answers, as fast as I could write them down.

This little incident set me thinking. While my attention was directed to something entirely different, another part of my mind had been working on that crossword. It remembered the clues and it produced the answers; it did for me what my conscious thought had been unable to do.

## Stimulating the Creative Faculty

I began looking for other writers' comments on this process, and I began experimenting with it myself. I found that everyone has this creative faculty, but that many people are unaware of it. I worked out a set of rules for stimulating the creative faculty. Here they are:

1. Consciously study the problem, whatever it may be, that you need to solve. Specify clearly what new idea or combination of ideas you need. The best way is to set the problem down in writing. For example: "What's the clearest way to explain so-and-so?"

2. Leave that question or problem in your subconscious; forget it for a while. Turn your attention away to some other piece of work, or to some noncreative activity, some nonwork subject.

3. You cannot tell when the answer, the creative idea, will come— it may be in a few minutes, it may be in hours or days. But whenever it does come, catch the idea and write it down.

Today I went out for lunch to a restaurant. Walking home, I suddenly got a useful idea for this book. I immediately stopped, whipped out my notebook, and wrote down the idea. Now that I'm back home, I can't for the life of me remember what it was. I've seen a lot of things and talked to several people in the meantime. That idea would be as good as lost if I didn't know that it's safely down on paper. Now I've looked at it, and see that it's something important for Chapter 11.

So keep a notebook with you *all the time* you are awake; and keep a notebook beside the bed while you sleep, because often you'll wake in the night with an idea. Don't think "Oh, that's so good I'll be sure to remember it in the morning. I'll write it down then." That's no use; the idea will almost certainly have evaporated by morning.

If you wake in the morning with a useful idea, don't think "I'll jot that down when I get settled at my desk." By the time you reach your desk, the idea will probably have disappeared. Always catch the idea promptly, and begin to write. You'll often find that there's more of it than you thought. You can keep on writing as new developments, new aspects of it come easily to mind. I have often written two pages of notes on one nighttime inspiration.

---

**Exercise 10:11**

Get a notebook and begin to use it. Write down some problem or question concerning your work. Review it occasionally. Watch for useful ideas; promptly write them in the book.

---

4. Another useful means of stimulating creativity is to experiment with various methods and routines of work, to find which suit you best.

For many people there are daily cycles, regular swings from maximum to minimum creativity. For some, morning is the best time; for others night is best. Neither I nor anyone else can tell you the details of your creativity cycle. You must discover them for yourself.

For some people, the physical means of setting down the first draft makes a big difference. Some do it best on the typewriter, others prefer a pen and paper.

Different working postures suit different people. Some prefer walking, talking into a tape recorder or making frequent stops for note taking. Some write standing up, at a high desk or lectern. Some relax, lying on a couch with a tape recorder or clipboard. Some write in the bathtub.

Facing another way may make a difference to your writing. I used to have my desk facing a big window with a marvelous view. I have now turned my desk around so that I face an inside wall; I find that in this position I get more work done.

Some writers have favorite clothes for work. I always wear the same pair of brown pants; they will last me for many years yet. Benjamin Disraeli always wrote wearing full evening dress—white tie and tails; he felt the clothes influenced his style for the better.

Some writers like to have certain kinds of music playing as they think or write or type.

It's worth experimenting with different methods and routines, to find what is best for you. But don't be impatient. Give it time, just as you would when starting on a new diet or a new fitness program. Persevere, not for one day or one week, but at least for a month. Then, if you are beginning to see results, go on; keep applying whatever method will make your writing easier and better.

---

### Exercise 10:12

Staring at a blank page, with no idea what to write, is an unpleasant experience. Here is a way to get started.

Begin: "I am preparing to write on . . . [name whatever aspect of your subject concerns you at the moment]. One of the most important words in this part of my script is going to be _____ which I would define as _____ . Some readers may not understand this term, because of _____ . Therefore I shall have to explain _____ , etc."

Presto! You have started writing!

---

### The Two Faculties Cooperate

That creative faculty is a bit temperamental, like a delicate machine. But if you consciously pamper it and encourage it, it will work wonders for you. Although you can consciously think about only one thing at a time, the creative faculty can be working on several different problems simultaneously.

By noting and using the products of the creative faculty, you are *rewarding* it. Think of it as a clever pet, which likes to see its offerings accepted. By rewarding your creative faculty, you make it *work harder*, because the act that is regularly rewarded is going to be more often and more efficiently performed.

Try, by experiment and practice, to get your rational and creative faculties working effectively and regularly together. When that habit of cooperation is consolidated, then you are really a writer!

## Summary

The problem: to verbalize skills and tastes.
Make comprehensive, detailed notes on:
    Materials and equipment
    Working conditions
    Overcoming difficulties
    Past successes
Make *plenty* of notes.
Be content with rough first drafts.
Divide draft material into convenient units.

A flexible page-numbering system greatly facilitates drafting and rewriting.

Control wordage, from first draft on.

Form the habit of rapid, piecemeal rewriting.

Prepare for indexing well in advance.

Proofreading and indexing can be contracted out.

The conscious mind gathers facts, asks questions.

The creative faculty produces ideas, solves problems.

Catch ideas and promptly write them down.

Experiment with different working conditions.

Train the two faculties to regular cooperation.

# 11

# Research

The craft of nonfiction writing is based upon research. Especially in how-to books and articles, you must give specific details to support every statement you make.

"A chair should, ideally, suit the physique of the person who is going to use it. So design your chairs accordingly."

That's sound theory, but so vague as to be useless for the would-be furniture maker. It does not say what parts of the user's anatomy are to be measured, nor how the chair dimensions should relate to those human dimensions.

Research gives you the precise facts—the weights, measures, numbers, costs, procedural details, etc.—that will transform vague statements into useful instruction.

Thorough research helps give you and your writing that authority I mentioned in Chapter 1, the authority that compels belief from readers and stifles attacks by critics. Dr. D. C. Jarvis did twenty years' research before writing his great how-to book, *Folk Medicine*.

I know a woman who has written and sold a brilliantly successful book on scuba diving. Now she is going to do a similar book on kayaking. Here is her research plan: (a) Spend one year learning how to kayak. (b) Spend three years writing magazine articles, interviewing experienced kayakers, getting advice, criticism, etc. (c) Then begin to plan the book.

Here are some hints for enjoyable, effective research:

# Reading

To be a good writer, you should be a steady reader. You should know as much as possible what has previously been written on your own subject. You also need a broad base of general knowledge to judge where you, with your past experience, your present skills, and your proposed writings, fit into the general scheme of things.

This knowledge, specialized and general, will make your own writing easier and better, and will greatly improve your prospects of selling it.

Yet, for a writer, reading can be a dangerous drug. Reading is so pleasurable! Reading takes up so much time! And reading is so much easier than writing!

You have passed the danger point when reading becomes *an excuse to postpone writing*. Only you can tell when you have reached that state. So be honest; be merciless with yourself. Do enough reading, but not too much!

## Periodicals

Systematically buy and read newspapers and magazines that contain information on your subject or subjects. It is impractical to store many whole copies of periodicals; so clip out items that may be useful to you.

Mark each clipping with the name of the publication it came from and the date of issue. Without that information, much of the value of a clipping is lost. For example, suppose you clip out an item about the discovery of a new process, ingredient, etc. Then, when you refer to the clipping later, you can't remember whether the "new" thing is six months, one year, or five years old!

File your clippings somehow. If you are planning a book, put each clipping in the appropriate chapter file. Or store them by subject divisions in big envelopes.

Clippings can be useful research material. But bear in mind that newspapers always, and magazines sometimes, are thrown together in haste; writers and editors may not have time to check everything for accuracy. So don't attach too much weight to those clippings. Whatever they tell you, try to get confirmation from other sources.

---

## Exercise 11:1

Start a system of taking and filing clippings from newspapers and magazines.

---

## Books

Build a collection of books about your own subject or subjects. Don't get only the new books as they appear; browse through used-book stores for old ones. They will contain much to deepen your knowledge and they may stir up some new ideas, too.

I don't like tearing pages out of a book; yet sometimes I want to have quick access to a passage that is important to me. So I mark the lines or paragraphs in the margin and turn down the corner of the page.

Also get some general reference books—almanacs, yearbooks, encyclopedias, etc. From such sources you can often find information that is not in the specialized, single-subject books—when and by whom some product or process was discovered or invented, political and economic forces that have caused changes in the use and function of various materials and products, current statistics on cost and consumption, etc.

Knowing such things is part of your qualification as a presumed expert on your subject. Well-selected reference books will give you that knowledge.

Don't overlook your telephone directory as a source of information. You want to interview experts? Most of them have telephones. Some thoughtful searching in the Yellow Pages can lead you to the right people. Look under the heading of whatever art, craft, trade, or profession you want.

Also look under closely related headings. For example, my Yellow Pages list no weavers; but they do show some weaving equipment suppliers, which might be good places to begin inquiries on the subject.

There are several pages of associations and clubs, many of which deal with how-to subjects as diverse as judo, public speaking, and tennis. Through such organizations you can meet experts and find out what they know; you can talk to beginners and find out what they want to know. (Valuable material for the how-to writer!)

---

**Exercise 11:2**

Compile a list of the specialized and general reference books you need. Establish some system for getting them soon.

---

# Libraries

I have found, over years of teaching night school courses, that many writers do not make full use of library facilities that are available to them. Here are some ideas:

### Indexes and Catalogs

To save time in directing your research, consult the indexes and catalogs. The main book index—probably on cards—and the departmental book indexes list the books the library holds by title, author, and subject. This book, for example, will be indexed under its title; there will also be a card headed "Hull, Raymond" and probably a card headed "Authorship" as well.

A book title alone will be insufficient as a guide; it obviously cannot tell all a book contains. You'll see that several digits of the index number are common to all books on the subject you want. Locate the shelf bearing those digits, and browse among the books there to find exactly what you want.

There are a number of other valuable indexes, published in book form. Here are the more important ones:

The *Subject Guide to Books in Print,* annually updated, lists all books currently in print, classified by subject. "In print," as the term is used here, means that a book is still kept in stock by its publisher and, if you want, can be ordered through a retail bookstore. (When a publisher lets a book go "out of print," he no longer lists it in his catalog. Any copies he has left over will probably be sold cheaply to firms operating cut-price or "remainder" bookstores.)

The *Cumulative Book Index,* in many thick volumes, lists all books that have been published. Most of the books will be out of print; but some of those may be found in libraries or used-book stores. There are some used-book dealers who specialize in obtaining hard-to-find books.

The *Library of Congress Catalog of Books by Subjects* is a multivolume set, periodically updated, showing all books held by the Library of Congress. This index, because of the way it is classified, may lead you to out-of-print books on your subject that your own library does not hold. Then, perhaps, you can borrow them through an interlibrary loan service (ask your librarian about this) or buy them through those specialized used-book stores.

The *Readers' Guide to Periodical Literature* is an annual series of books, indexing published magazine articles by subject and author.

The *New York Times Index* lists articles published in that newspaper by subject and by author; each entry gives the date, page, and column of the article cited. Many entries give summaries of the articles' contents, too. The *Index* is bound in annual volumes and is updated with biweekly and quarterly supplements. For full instructions on its use, see *Guide to the Incomparable New York Times Index,* by Grant W. Morse.

## Periodicals

Most libraries have a good selection of magazines. These may help you decide which periodicals you would like to subscribe to. Also, you can use library copies of the periodicals you cannot afford to or don't care to buy regularly.

### Microfilm

Many libraries have big stocks of assorted material, including back issues of magazines and newspapers, stored on microfilm and available for reading on the premises.

---

### Exercise 11:3

Make a visit to your library for the specific purpose of getting familiar with the system of indexes, catalogs, and microfilmed periodicals.

---

### Librarians

Librarians have an intimate knowledge of their stock and facilities. They are there to help you; they will respond enthusiastically to polite, intelligent queries.

The main reference desk is the place to begin if you don't know your way around the library. Simply tell the librarians what you want to find out; they will tell you where to look. Departmental and section librarians will give detailed information on their own specialties.

### Notes and Copies

Take ample writing material on every trip to the library. When you are researching in a book, note the title, author, and publisher, and the page from which each item of information is taken.

Most libraries have machines that make photocopies from books or magazines. If you are not sure how to work the machine, a librarian will show you how. If each photocopy sheet does not plainly identify the source, mark it at once; information loses much of its value if you don't know where it comes from.

### Saving Time

You can save time in library research by adapting the interview technique. Make a written list of the questions to which you are seeking answers. Also, as you do in an interview, go on to seek relevant information beyond the precise range of your questions. But beware of slipping into random reading—material that is interesting but not what you need. Research time is business!

## Other Sources

I have in my desk a file labeled "Misc. Writing Records." Among its contents are several sheets of names and addresses. Many people and organizations have in the past given me expert information on various subjects; I may want to consult them again sometime.

Build your own list of potential informants. Watch your newspaper for names of people who might be useful—not the visiting celebrities but the editors of various specialized sections of the paper. Who are the secretaries of local art and craft organizations? Who are the curators of museums? Who runs the information or PR service at the university or college? Who runs the local bookstores, new and used?

What if you phone someone for information and find he doesn't have what you need? Make a point of asking "Can you suggest someone else who might be able to help me?" This question, regularly asked, will usually lead you to the person you need.

If you intend to do much serious writing on a subject, develop the habit of keeping your mind—somewhat like a radio—always "tuned in" to the subject. You will find intermittent showers of material coming your way from unexpected sources. When such material arrives, don't simply think "My, my! That's interesting!" Take hold of the new material, *write it down*, and *use it*.

The act of using one batch of material sharpens your receptivity and improves your prospects for obtaining more.

---

### Exercise 11:4

Open your own "Miscellaneous Writing Records" file and begin gathering material for it.

---

## Questionnaires

You can often get a body of exclusive, up-to-date information by issuing questionnaires aimed at ordinary people, nonexperts. You will probably not want to bother with questionnaires for specialized, technical subjects like How to Operate a Slide Rule, How to Repair Locks, or How to Dowse for Water and Metals. But for subjects of wider appeal—How to Raise Healthy, Happy Children, How to Develop Your Occult Powers, How to Win Money at Cards, for example—questionnaires might be very useful.

Here are the sorts of things you can find out:

(a) What does the man-in-the-street already know or think about your subject? (It's useful to find out how many true and false ideas on it are in circulation. That will help you plan and write better.)

(b) Where did he get his information, true or false?

(c) What would he *like* to know about the subject? (More valuable guidance. The customer is always right!)

(d) Money and the subject: What have people been spending on it? What are they spending now? What would they like to spend on it?

(e) Changes in the subject: Do they think it should be altered, improved, made bigger or smaller, made the way it used to be, etc?

(f) Popularity: What proportion of people own it, or use it, or do it? What ratio of males to females are among owners, users? What are the proportions among various age groups?

(g) Durability: How many say that it is being, or should be, or will be, replaced by something else?

(h) Anecdotes: Ask for personal experiences, pleasant or unpleasant, with the subject.

It is worth spending the time and effort to draw up a really good questionnaire.

## Format

A questionnaire should occupy one side of a standard 8½x11-inch (22x28-cm) sheet of paper. Many people feel reluctant to fill in anything longer or more complex than that.

The text of the questionnaire can be typed single-spaced.

1. Opening statement. Begin with something like this: "I am researching the subject of so-and-so. I would appreciate your answers to the following questions. Names will not be used."

[Your typed signature.]

The statement "Names will not be used" reassures some people who might otherwise be reluctant to put their ideas on paper.

2. Questions. Type the questions. For some you may be able to put answers—Yes, No, Often, Sometimes, Once, Never, 1-10, 10-100, 100-1,000, etc.—leaving space for checkmarks. For others you will need to leave space for a written reply.

3. After the questions, put a note: "If you have any further comments on the subject, please use reverse side."

4. At the bottom, leave space for a signature; if it is relevant, add: "Sex: F_____ M_____."

Review the draft of your questionnaire daily for about five days to be sure it is what you need. Then have some copies made. I usually get 250 copies; you can estimate how many you will need.

Fold the copies, put them in stamped, self-addressed envelopes, and start handing them out, preferably to the sort of people who might be expected to be interested in the book.

## Results

With a little care in selecting the people I give questionnaires to, I usually receive a return rate of about 30 percent to 40 percent, 80 to 100 replies out of 250. Most respondents simply answer the questions. A few accept the invitation to add comments of their own; this gives valuable extra material, some of it quite unforeseen.

Total the results; calculate the percentage of each reply to a question where applicable.

Now, what significance can you attach to these results? You have not made an accurate nationwide survey of experience or opinion on the subject—and you should not say, or imply, in the text of the book that you have. Don't say "35 percent of the population say that they have never . . ." or "75 percent of women would like to see. . . ." Such assertions are not justified; they may expose you and your book to serious criticism. Think carefully about what you have found out and use the material discreetly.

---

### Exercise 11:5

Draw up a trial questionnaire. Make just a few copies, perhaps ten. Hand them out to see what people think, know, or would like to know about your subject.

---

# Interviewing

Even if you are an expert in your subject, you'll benefit by talking to other experts. For some kinds of subjects you will want to interview nonexperts, ordinary citizens. What do they know, or think, about the subject or product? What would they like to see improved?

Good interviewing technique will produce the information you need. Poorly conducted interviews are a waste of time, for you and the interviewee.

### Appointments

For most serious interviews it's best to make appointments. Telephone several days in advance.

(a) Give your name.

(b) Identify yourself as a writer.

(c) State exactly the subject of your writing project.

(d) If you have a contract or a definite expression of interest from some book or magazine publisher, mention that fact.

(e) If you want to take photographs of the interviewee, or of anything he makes or owns, ask permission in advance. Many people will want to smarten themselves up or dust off and rearrange their property for the camera.

If you're not accustomed to such negotiations, you'll find that it helps to prepare a written script of what you want to say. Here, for example, might be your script in asking for an interview with a famous writer:

"Mr. Booker, my name is Verity Scrivener; I'm an author. I'm writing a book for Drywall and Pledge Press on 'How to Lick the Drinking Habit.' May I have an interview with you, about some alcoholic writers you've known and how they did, or did not, conquer the habit?"

(That is the opening you have prepared and written down. Now let us see how the conversation goes on.)

"Hm! I don't know about that, Ms. Scrivener. It's a rather delicate subject."

"Mr. Booker, whatever I write based on our interview I'll check with you before sending it in."

(This promise will sometimes reassure potential interviewees. Perhaps they have been interviewed before and misquoted; perhaps that's why they are nervous now.

I am aware that some writers and editors don't like the practice of checking back with interviewees. Pressure of time usually prevents it in newspaper work anyway; but for book or magazine work I usually offer it.

The checkup can also ensure accuracy. Even with the best of intentions, you may have made a mistake! It's better to catch the mistake during the research process than to have it noticed—and rightly criticized—when the book or article is in print.

"Well . . . all right, then."

"Thank you, Mr. Booker. May I suggest Monday or Tuesday of next week?"

"Tuesday would be OK for me."

"Tuesday, then. Morning or afternoon?"

"Tuesday at 10 a.m."

"Tuesday, 10 a.m." (You are writing this down as you speak!) "And one more thing, Mr. Booker. I'd like to get photographs of you and of your famous liquor-bottle collection." (This speech, too, could be scripted in advance.)

"Very good! I'll get a haircut on Monday. Don't want to look like one of these damned hippies! Ha-ha! See you next Tuesday, Ms. Scrivener."

Notice how the writer offered a choice of dates. This is always better than suggesting just one date. It's also a polite way of suggesting that you would like the interview *soon*, not just some time in the future. If the interviewee does not specify a time, lead up to it by the same "choice offering" technique. Ask "nine or ten o'clock?" and so proceed to setting an exact time.

If you are trying to get information from big organizations, public or private, ask for the PR department, information officer, and such people; they can tell you whom to see, and will often set up the interviews for you.

## Preparation

Thorough preparation is the basis for smooth-running, productive interviews.

1. Find out in advance as much as you can about the interviewee. You look stupid if you have to ask such trifles as how he spells his name! In big organizations, receptionists and secretaries can give such information.

You may be able to find useful material in Who's Who books, directories, library clipping files, and other relevant sources.

By tactfully showing that you know a lot about the interviewee—for example, by a reference to some long-past accomplishment—you can deliver a graceful compliment. The more you know about a person, the easier it is to conduct an interview.

2. You should have at least a fair general knowledge of the subject in order to ask the right questions and understand the answers you receive. For that reason it can sometimes be wise to leave interviewing till a fairly late stage of your research program. At least be familiar with the pronunciation, meaning, and spelling of technical terms that are likely to be used.

---

### Exercise 11:6

If you have an interview coming up, write out:
  (a) Personal notes on the interviewee
  (b) List of technical terms

---

3. Make a list of questions that you want to ask. Carefully pick out one that you think will be best to lead off with. It should be something that you feel pretty sure the person can answer easily, something that will get the interview off to a smooth, pleasant start. Here are some ideas:

(a) A question about the origins or discovery or invention of the subject. Suppose you were interviewing me about how-to writing. You might ask, "Mr. Hull, what is the oldest one in your collection of how-to books?"

(b) The start of the interviewee's own connection with the subject, e.g., "Mr. Hull, just how and when did you first get involved with how-to writing?"

(c) Some current incident or condition relevant to the subject: "Mr. Hull, what's the reason for the recent boom in how-to writing?"

In any subject, try to find and bring out the elements of *conflict*. By "conflict" I do not necessarily mean person-to-person disputes (though sometimes those may be involved). I mean the difficulties, delays, doubts, problems, mistakes, dangers, etc., that are involved in every kind of constructive or creative process.

Don't simply ask "What raw materials and equipment do you need?" but "What problems do you face in getting good raw materials and equipment?"

Don't simply ask "What is your theory about so-and-so?" Also ask "What are the rival theories? Who holds them? What's wrong with them?" Not only "How did you get started in so-and-so?" but also "What obstacles did you encounter in starting . . . advancing . . . perfecting . . . , etc?"

Thorough coverage of the conflict in a subject will create interest for readers; it will be helpful for them, because they are likely to encounter the same conflicts themselves.

Lead up gradually to the most difficult or controversial subjects: "Mr. Hull, what do you think about writing books on such subjects as How to Commit Suicide, How to Perform an Abortion, or How to Execute the Perfect Murder?"

It is best to save such things till late in the interview, when the subject's ideas are flowing freely and he is talking fluently.

Have all your questions neatly typed out on a sheet or sheets that will fit in your notebook.

4. Have good writing equipment. Carry two pens; it's humiliating if you have to borrow a pen from the interviewee!

Carry a notebook with stiff covers; a stenographer's pad is good. Then you can write on your knee while sitting, or you can write standing up while the expert shows you around his laboratory, workshop, or factory.

You certainly should not expect to spread loose papers on the expert's desk or table while you write. Moreover, if you use loose sheets of paper, you can easily drop or forget some of them; with a notebook you are sure of taking all your material away.

---

**Exercise 11:7**

Type out all the questions you can think of for your interview. Choose one to serve as the opener.

---

**Dress**

Be discreet, be practical, in dressing for an interview. The first thing about you that the interviewee notices will be your clothing, so choose a style that will not alienate him, and that will suit the place. Clothes that are appropriate in the living room of a wealthy book collector would be out of place for an interview beside a creek with a gold prospector.

## Punctuality

Be punctual for an interview! If the interviewee is an expert or an authority you should assume that his time is worth more than yours. Even if that's not the case, punctuality is a form of courtesy. Bear in mind that "punctual" means "on time." Half an hour early can be as annoying as half an hour late.

If you need to pass doorkeepers, receptionists, or the like, a printed business card will speed your introduction and admission.

## Be Businesslike

In conducting an interview, there is seldom any need to start discussing weather, health, politics, or other such common subjects of casual conversation. Get down to business promptly.

I usually begin, "Mr. X, as you'll remember, I want to get some information from you about . . .," or " . . . I want to get some expert advice from you about. . . ."

A speech of twenty to thirty seconds, ending in that preselected first question, will usually get the ball rolling. If you feel the least bit doubtful about your ability to begin, write out your opening speech in full and memorize it.

Don't bother an interviewee for bits of information, such as statistics, which you can easily get from reference books.

Don't be afraid! Most people *enjoy* talking about themselves or their specialties; they are *flattered* to be *intelligently* interviewed.

Try to be polite throughout, even if the interviewee is not.

## Enrichment

Work through your list of questions, checking them off as you go. But bear in mind that those questions are only based on *your* ideas! The interview will be richer, more productive, if you can lead the interviewee on to talk freely, beyond simply answering your questions.

Some fluent talkers will do that without any persuasion. But with people who are shy and unaccustomed to giving interviews, you may have to use some tactics.

Ask the interviewee to show you his workshop, tools and equipment, the things he makes, his photographs, models, or whatever exhibits are relevant. For this purpose, it is obviously best to conduct interviews at the expert's own home, office, workshop, laboratory, etc. If possible, get him to give you a demonstration of his specialty; take detailed notes on how he does it.

This sort of exhibiting and demonstrating may set a shy person talking. But you should always ask for it in any case. The workshop, materials, etc., are commonplace to the expert; he may not even think to show them if you don't ask!

Moreover, if you keep your eyes open, you can learn a lot about the interviewee from the arrangement, adequacy, cleanliness, apparent efficiency or inefficiency, etc., of his workplace.

Here is the best place to take photographs, if you want them. Be sure, in workshops, laboratories, and such places, that there is no danger of explosion from bursting flashbulbs. Some people may offer to supply photographs of themselves. Beware of wooden-looking, posed studio portraits—editors don't like them, and neither do readers. An action shot is best.

If you don't photograph him, make a point of noting a brief, vivid description of the interviewee. If you can't conveniently do it during the interview, pause somewhere and do it soon after you leave.

### Time Saving

Suppose you want to interview a busy person who offers to allow you just a short time. Give him your typed list of questions. He can read the questions faster than you can speak them. As he replies, note his answers on sheets containing the same questions, laid out with plenty of space between them.

### Notes vs. Tapes

Some writers favor tape-recording interviews. Taping offers the advantage of a verbatim report and lets you keep your eye on the interviewee most of the time. But it does have disadvantages. You can never be quite sure that the machine is working properly. Shy, nervous people may be intimidated by speaking into a microphone. A long interview will have to be interrupted as you turn over or change tapes. And the presence of a tape recorder discourages off-the-record remarks, which, although they are not to be quoted, can sometimes deepen your understanding of a subject.

Shorthand, too, will give you a verbatim report of an interview; but few writers nowadays can do it. The fact is that you do not need a verbatim report of an interview. One newspaper editor I heard of would not let his reporters use shorthand on the theory that "All you can get in longhand is all you need." On this principle, you summarize the major ideas that the interviewee propounds, and you note verbatim a few key phrases that are especially important.

If you do use a tape recorder, take writing materials as well, for use if the machine fails.

### Editing

When you write up your script, you will have to do a good deal of editing, certainly through two drafts, and maybe through three or four. Carefully separate what is important and relevant to your subject from what is merely curious.

In reporting quotes, you can polish up the sentences a bit where necessary. Don't put in all the er's and ah's; cut the repetitions and unimportant phrases; correct the grammar where necessary.

You are certainly not obliged to report all that the interviewee says, but you should represent his opinions and accomplishments fairly.

An interviewee may tell you certain things if you agree that they are "off the record." That means that he does not want to be quoted as the source of those particular items.

Bear that in mind when editing. Off-the-record material may be useful to you as background knowledge that helps you understand the subject better. Or maybe you can include it in your book or article without ascribing it to anyone in particular. "Recent research indicates that . . ."; "Some authorities suggest that . . ."—such expressions as these will provide the necessary camouflage.

It's generally considered unethical for a writer not to honor such an off-the-record promise. Keep in mind that you want to build a reputation for being honest and reliable. If you double-cross one informant he will probably spread the word around; then you will find it becoming harder and harder to get good interviews with experts in that field.

## Practice

Don't invite embarrassment, and risk failure, by having your first interview with some important stranger. Practice a few times under easy conditions. Interview a few people who are not too awe-inspiring—friends, members of your writers' club or craft club, or anyone else who will cooperate.

---

### Exercise 11:8

Conduct some practice interviews. Carefully write up and edit your reports. Go over them with the interviewees, checking for fairness and accuracy.

Try to get the cooperation of another writer. Interview each other on some subject the interviewee knows well.

If possible, find someone to act the role of "shy interviewee" and give brief, precise answers. Practice leading him on to talk freely.

---

### Payment

Most people do not expect to be paid for an interview. So, when asking for an appointment, do not raise the question of payment. If someone comes flat out and demands a fee for an interview, you must quickly calculate whether the desired information would be worth the price.

Sometimes, if there is no particular reason for going to the interviewee's home or workshop, you can arrange to meet him at a hotel or restaurant; then you buy him a meal or a few drinks as he talks. If you pay the bill in cash, get and keep a check stub or receipt from the cashier.

When I am going to such a fee-paying interview, I prepare two typed copies (each on a half-sheet of paper) of a receipt. It looks something like this:

RECEIVED

from Raymond Hull, as fee for consultation on [name the subject], the sum of _____ dollars. Dated this nth day of [month & year].

EXPERT'S NAME IN CAPITALS

Signed _____

With such a blank form, you are ready in case the expert wants payment in cash. Fill in the details and have him sign; give him one copy and keep one for yourself.

If he accepts a check, then the canceled check serves as your receipt.

One way or another, in such dealings get *written records*. Such costs, if legitimately incurred in research for your writing, will be tax-deductible expenses.

## Instruction Courses

Although you may already be an expert in your subject, there is still much to be gained from instruction courses—night school and summer school—from lectures, seminars, conferences, etc.

(a) Register and sit in as a member of the class or audience. Every subject is in a state of constant flux; new materials and new technical procedures are being discovered; public taste is changing.

You are never too old or too experienced to learn! There is also a powerful stimulus in rubbing shoulders with eager beginners. There are valuable contacts to be made, contacts that may help you produce and sell more and better work. You will benefit, too, by the chance to size up your competition, i.e., the instructors, lecturers, etc.

(b) Be a teacher. Set up a course yourself. Advertise, obtain students, hold classes. Take individual pupils for private instruction sessions. Or find some existing adult education system and offer them your services. As an adult education teacher, your earnings will probably be less, but so will your responsibilities and worries.

Teaching a subject requires a constant polishing and widening of one's knowledge of it; that is why I have put this item in this chapter.

# Copyright

This is a good place to mention the subject of copyright as it applies to books. In plain, nonlegal terms, copyright means an author's ownership of his work, and his right to control and profit by its printing, reproduction, or use in any other medium.

The copyright of this book is mine, because I wrote it. I have, in effect, leased exclusively to Writer's Digest Books the right to print it and sell it.

Copyright law varies somewhat in different countries, but a common rule is that copyright endures through the author's life and for fifty years after his death.

For example, suppose you are gathering material to use in a book on how to write poetry. You can quite safely quote all you want from Walt Whitman; he died in 1892 and his work is "out of copyright," or (another phrase that means the same thing) "in the public domain." But you would need to obtain permission for reproducing a piece from the Poet's Corner of your local newspaper; that poet is still alive and writing!

## Dangers in Copyright

Many would-be writers are unaware of the risks they run in copyright violations. A writer once brought to me, for criticism, the rough draft of a book she had just finished. About half the total wordage consisted of photocopied chunks from other people's books, glued in between passages of her own writing.

"Have you got permission from all the writers to use their work?" I asked.

"I didn't think that would be necessary," she replied. "I assumed they would be glad to have the publicity."

Don't make any such assumptions! If you want to quote from other writers, and if you have the least suspicion that the material may still be under copyright, then check.

The way to do that is to write to the publisher of the book. Say what you are doing, enclose a copy of the passage(s) you want, and ask permission to use it/them. You may be refused; maybe you will get the permission free; or you may have to pay for it.

I mentioned earlier the need to mark the source on every item you copy verbatim from other people's writings. If you don't do so, six months, a year, or two years later you may forget where it came from and think that it was a clever little piece you wrote yourself. You'll put it in your book and, Bingo! the process server will be knocking at your door.

I stress the need for great care in this matter. Copyright violation can land you, and your publisher, in severe legal and financial trouble; it can badly injure your reputation as a writer.

Published illustrations are also likely to be protected by copyright. You should get permission—just as you would for a passage of text—if you want to reproduce them.

## Wide Open

There are some things that cannot be copyrighted.

1. You cannot copyright *an idea*. For example, you can take the *idea* of a book on writing how-to material, and write another book about it. So long as you do not use the same form of words as mine, I shall have no grounds for complaint.

For example: Suppose you have a brilliant idea for a book. You talk about it at your writers' club and another member writes a book on the idea and sells it before yours is ready. That may impair the market for your book; but still, you have no redress. The law protects not an idea, but the precise arrangement of words in which an idea is expressed.

2. You cannot copyright a title. There are so many potential book subjects and so few words in the typical title that, over the years, some duplication of titles is inevitable. Still, try to be original; avoid famous titles. Putting your name in the title, if it seems appropriate, will give you a degree of exclusivity. A glance at my bookshelf shows a couple of good examples: *Gayelord Hauser's Treasury of Secrets*, by Gayelord Hauser, and *Lasker's Manual of Chess*, by Dr. Emmanuel Lasker.

3. You cannot copyright information that is generally known. For example, a list of the melting points of metals, the multiplication tables, a list of mountains arranged in order of height, a chart of the calorie values of foodstuffs.

4. The words which a person speaks to you impromptu, as in an interview, cannot be copyrighted. You may quote them verbatim.

---

### Exercise 11:9

Examine the Exemplary Dozen for information about copyright:

(a) Find the main copyright notice for each book.

(b) Look for any acknowledgments of the use of copyrighted material from other authors.

---

## Summary

Research: the basis of nonfiction writing.
For interviewing:
    Make an appointment, offering choice of dates and times.
    Find out about the interviewee in advance.
    Prepare yourself on the subject.
    Type out all your questions.
    Look for the conflict within the subject.
    Be punctual and businesslike.
    Lead the interviewee to talk freely.
    Ask for practical demonstrations.
    Practice interviewing in easy conditions.
Reading for research:
    Read enough, but not too much.
    Regularly clip newspapers, magazines.
    Collect useful books.
    Use the phone book.
Library research:
    Use indexes and catalogs.
    Consult librarians.
    Note origin of all material.
    Use all possible sources
Check copyright of all material quoted.
Get permission where necessary.
Try questionnaires for opinion sampling.
Taking or teaching courses is instructive.

# 12

# Style: How to Make Them Understand

Many a writer's success or failure is determined by the style of his writing. It's not enough to have expert knowledge; it's not enough to have the perseverance to put what you know on paper. You must also have the skill to write in a way that will tempt people to read, keep them reading, and make them understand what you have written.

Fashion helps to determine what is considered good style or bad style at any time. Some famous old how-to books were written in styles that would be unacceptable today. Here, for example, is a sample from *The Chess-Player's Handbook* by Howard Staunton, published in 1875:

> With every allowance for the amazing disparity in the importance of the individuals and the magnitude of the objects at stake, there is an analogy observable, too, in the abilities required for the command of armies and the perfectly first-rate manoeuvring of the mimic warriors of the chess-board. The commander of an army must possess no less a profound acquaintance with the general principles which regulate the conduct of a long and tedious campaign than with those that are called into requisition in actual conflict. He must be able equally to arrange the plan of preliminary operations—to act at once and with decision in cases of the most pressing emer-

gency, and on the occurrence of the most unforeseen events—
to judge the importance of a position and of the strength of an
intrenchment—to discover from the slightest indications the
designs of the enemy, while his own are impenetrable—and at
the same time to preside with unshaken self-possession over
the tumult of the battle-field, and the raging fury of an assault.
The qualifications of a really finished chess-player, however
less in degree, are somewhat similar in kind.

The many long words, the convoluted sentence structure, the pro-
fusion of adjectives—these produce what would today be called a
windy, oratorical style.

A present-day writer might say, "Some board games give their
players the vicarious experience of obstacle racing, investing, spy-
ing, playacting, golfing, jailbreaking, or space travel; chess simu-
lates war."

Instead of belaboring one point in two hundred words, the modern
writer would thus make two points in less than twenty-five!

Good how-to writing should be clear, concise, accurate, and interesting. Here is an exercise to help you attain those qualities:

## Exercise 12:1

The following paragraph is from the introductory portion of Edgar
Allan Poe's "The Philosophy of Composition." Express the same
ideas in good contemporary style.

I have often thought how interesting a magazine paper might
be written by an author who would—that is to say, who
could—detail, step by step, the processes by which one of his
compositions attained its ultimate point of completion. Why
such a paper has never been given to the world, I am much at a
loss to say—but perhaps the authorial vanity has had more to
do with the omission than any other one cause. Most writers—
poets in especial—prefer having it understood that they compose by a species of fine frenzy—an ecstatic intuition—and
would positively shudder at letting the public take a peep behind the scenes, at the elaborate and vacillating crudities of
thought—at the true purposes seized only at the last moment—
at the innumerable glimpses of ideas that arrived not at the ma-
turity of full view—at the fully-matured fancies discarded in
despair as unmanageable—at the cautious selections and rejections—at the painful erasures and interpolations—in a word, at
the wheels and pinions, the tackle for scene-shifting, the step-
ladders and demon-traps, the cock's feathers, the red paint and

black patches, which, in ninety-nine cases out of the hundred, constitute the properties of the literary *histrio*.

## Be Clear

"Clear" writing is easily understood on the first reading. More than that, it cannot be *mis*understood!

For example, in a child's handicraft book a writer might say "Turn the screw clockwise to tighten it, counterclockwise to loosen it." That was once clear enough, but not nowadays. Many kids, raised on digital watches and clocks, are not sure what "clockwise" means! Someone has to figure out a substitute for that good old word.

This, then, is the point that must always be considered first: "What will be clear, or what could possibly be *unclear, to my readers?*"

I was talking this over with a friend who was writing a cookbook aimed at men with no knowledge of the subject. She remarked that it would be useless, for example, to say "fold in egg whites"; those readers would not know how to separate an egg white, let alone how to fold it in. Step-by-step instructions would be needed.

She wrote the phrase "If you think that the mixture is too stiff . . ." and then realized that a beginner would not know what was "too stiff." She had to explain it. It would be no good to tell those greenhorn cooks, "Remove from heat when done." She would have to describe exactly what the dish *looked* like and *smelled* like and *felt* like when it was "done."

This sort of problem constantly besets the expert writing how-to material for beginners. So whenever you put down something that readers may not understand, explain it *immediately*. (This is the reason each illustration should be as close as possible to the relevant text.)

### Vocabulary

Two aspects of this subject concern you as a how-to writer.

1. Do you have an ample vocabulary for the general purposes of writing? Ideas, as originally conceived in the mind, are nonverbal. Do you find, most of the time, that words appropriate to express your ideas spring to hand just about as fast as you can write or type them?

Be honest with yourself. If your vocabulary is inadequate, promptly start to enlarge it.

(a) Make sure that you fully understand every word you read. Get two or three dictionaries. Two or three are better than one; you'll find it instructive to see how dictionaries differ on spelling, meanings, pronunciations, and rules for usage. (N.B. Some publishers, in their writers' directory listings, in correspondence, or in "style sheets" sent out to writers, specify which dictionary they have chosen as their standard of correctness.)

(b) Get a thesaurus and/or a dictionary of synonyms and antonyms.

(c) Spend less time watching television and more time talking with literate, articulate people. Don't hesitate to ask people for the meanings of any words they use that you do not understand. Such a request will usually be taken as a compliment.

(d) Spend some time working crossword puzzles and other word quizzes difficult enough to make you think hard. Play word games such as Scrabble.

This systematic vocabulary development should be carried on year after year; consider it an integral part of the writer's business.

2. Do you have a complete, accurate technical vocabulary for whatever you are writing about? A person may have great practical expertise in some subject and yet not know all the relevant technical terms that are used by other experts hundreds or thousands of miles away. Publishers and readers have the right to expect that you will use words understood by everyone who knows the subject.

The way to check your technical vocabulary is by reading books, magazines, newspapers, and other sources of relevant information. This checking must be continual, because in most fields technical terms are changing; new materials and processes are being discovered; old materials and products are being renamed; former nicknames are becoming accepted as real names; old terms are falling out of fashion. (You would not now write, as Edgar Allan Poe did, about ". . . the literary *histrio*.")

### Sentence Length

Readers understand printed material better when it is broken into fairly short sentences. It is as if your eye pauses at each period, colon, or semicolon. You mentally chew over the chunk of information you have been given and digest it. Then you are ready to move ahead and look at the next chunk. Each pause is very brief, of course. The brain works fast. Still, those pauses do help in comprehension, absorption, and retention of the material.

Faced with a long, complicated sentence, a reader will keep plowing ahead, but having had no opportunity to pause and think, by the time he reaches the end he will have forgotten what the beginning was about.

This fact has only recently been acknowledged by writers. A writer's skill and taste used to be measured in part by length of the sentences he could construct without violating any of the rules of grammar. In Howard Staunton's piece, quoted at the start of this chapter, there are 195 words in four sentences; so the average sentence length is about 49 words. In the excerpt from Poe cited in Exercise 12:1 there are 213 words in three sentences, an average of 71 words per sentence.

I think in how-to writing an average of 15 words per sentence is a good target to aim at.

---

**Exercise 12:2**

Take random samples—ten consecutive sentences each—from the Exemplary Dozen books. Work out the average sentence length for each author.

---

**Exercise 12:3**

Take random ten-sentence samples from your own how-to writing and calculate the average sentence length. If the average is above 25 words, rewrite to get it down below 20.

Here are some hints for reducing the average length of your sentences:

(a) Eliminate waste wordage. (See "Be Concise" later in this chapter for hints on how to accomplish this.)

(b) Watch particularly for excessive use of conjunctions to tie together groups of ideas that could be more clearly expressed as separate sentences.

(c) Write "SHORTER SENTENCES" on a card and stick it on the wall over your desk.

(d) When reading books, magazines, or newspapers, occasionally pause and check sentence lengths. If you find an excessively long one, figure out how to shorten it.

Note that in this section I have talked about *average* sentence length. There is certainly no need to try to make *all* your sentences 15 words long, or whatever is your target figure. That would be boring! In most tunes the notes vary in length. You can use a similar principle in controlling sentence length. But if you find many of your sentences running beyond twice the average, take care! The habit of writing long-winded sentences can creep up on you.

**Paragraph Length**

A paragraph—it may consist of one sentence or several sentences—conveys a major unit of the subject matter.

N.B. That paragraph contained one sentence; but the same material could have been conveyed in two sentences:

"A paragraph conveys a major unit of the subject matter. It may consist of one sentence or several sentences."

I think the first format is better, for reasons I shall explain later in this chapter.

In old books you will often see a paragraph occupying half a page or more. That kind of format is not acceptable to modern readers. I would recommend keeping paragraphs down to an average of 50 words. As with sentences, don't try to make them all the same length. Variety adds interest to the visual and mental effect of the page. But if you find many of your paragraphs running on beyond 100 words, look for ways of breaking them up.

N.B. The previous paragraph contains 81 words. It is not grotesquely long, but it could advantageously have been broken at the end of the second sentence. Those first two sentences contained an important new idea. The paragraph break would have given you time—more time than was offered by the sentence break alone—to think over and absorb that idea before reading on.

---

### Exercise 12:4

Take random samples—ten consecutive paragraphs each—from the Exemplary Dozen books. Work out the average paragraph length for each author.

---

### Exercise 12:5

Take random ten-paragraph samples from your own how-to writing; calculate your average paragraph length. If the average is above 60 words, rewrite to get it down to around 50.

---

### Sentence Structure

"Not only the questions of vocabulary and sentence length, but also other, more subtle factors of sentence structure . . . "

There's the start of a badly constructed sentence! Those 18 words leave the reader with little or no idea of what the sentence is going to say. He is momentarily puzzled.

He does not *consciously* think "I don't understand this." Nevertheless, the impression is planted in his mind. If the process is repeated too often, the effect will become conscious.

"Not only the questions of vocabulary and sentence length, but also other, more subtle factors of sentence structure that help to produce clear writing must be considered." That's how the sentence could be completed.

There is a lot wrong with it. The phrase that reveals the point of the whole sentence—the *topic*—is "to produce clear writing." That topic and the verb "must be considered" are placed at the end. In effect, the sentence offers a long string of words whose significance is not immediately apparent; *only afterwards* does it explain what they are all about.

A good rule of effective sentence structure is to reveal the topic of a sentence without delay.

"Rather than carrying a bundle of loose paper, which will quite likely be awkward to handle, it has been found by many experienced writers that a notebook with stiff covers is rather more convenient, since it allows you to write in various positions."

There is another example of the obscure beginning, the "buried topic," and the rambling structure.

See how I actually wrote that material in Chapter 11: "Carry a notebook with *stiff covers;* a stenographer's pad is good. Then you can write on your knee while sitting, or you can write standing up while the expert shows you around his laboratory, workshop, or factory."

Avoid what I call "throat-clearing openings," the sprinkling around of vague expressions before getting to the point of the sentence. For example:

"It is not only . . . "

"As perhaps the best among several potentially good ways to . . ."

"It has sometimes been suggested that . . ."

"As some writers claim, there are advantages in . . ."

"In a certain number of cases, it has been found that . . ."

An *occasional* weak sentence opening may add variety, which is one element of a pleasing style. But oft-repeated moments of obscurity will leave readers feeling dissatisfied; oft-repeated "ahems" and hesitations will undermine your authority as expert on the subject.

---

**Exercise 12:6**

Analyze several pages of your own writing for structural weakness in the sentences:

Buried topics

Weak openings

---

**Punctuation**

Be generous with punctuation marks—periods, colons, semicolons, commas, dashes, and exclamation marks. An old school of thought implied that these marks were somehow like props and patches, so heavy use of them showed that the underlying structure was defective.

Not so! I mentioned earlier the advantage of writing in short sentences. Sentences can be further clarified by appropriate use of minor punctuation marks to break down ideas into smaller, coherent units of meaning. Abundant use of punctuation marks also tends to give your page a pleasing touch of visual variety.

## Exercise 12:7

Check your script to see where it might be made clearer by a more generous use of punctuation marks.

## Titles and Headings

Chapter titles, subheads, captions for illustrations, and all other such headings must convey their message to the reader *instantly*. Keep thinking of this as you write them.

## Exercise 12:8

Check your titles, subheads, and other headings for clarity.

# Be Accurate

As I mentioned in Chapter 8, some how-to writers deliberately introduce errors into the instructions they offer. That is done so readers will not be able to duplicate the fancy effects that the author proudly shows in the illustrations as his own work.

"Too bad!" thinks the reader. "I guess I'm just not quite good enough. I'll have to stick to easier projects in the future."

An author may get away with such deceptions when neither the editor nor the average reader can tell right from wrong in the technical material. But I suggest that an author who does such a thing is a scoundrel! There is a relationship of trust between reader and writer that should not be violated.

Sooner or later a publisher will find out what such a writer has been up to, and will not want any more of his books.

Moreover, the book publishing business is fairly close-knit. The people who work in it know each other; they eat, drink, and gossip together. Word of such dirty tricks can spread fast; soon the unscrupulous writer will find that no one wants to publish his books at all.

## Extravagant Claims

After a few years of night school teaching, a writer decides to write a textbook. In the outline he claims, "I have taught people of all ages and all professions."

*All* ages? *All* professions? Surely it would be more accurate to say "people from the teens to the seventies, and from many different walks of life . . ."

Beware of "ultimate" words and expressions—"the best," "the worst," "the greatest," "the cheapest," "never," "always," "inevitably," "entirely," "without the slightest shadow of doubt," "the entire human race," "every normal civilized person," etc.

We may use such expressions loosely in conversation to make our remarks more emphatic, more convincing. And I don't say they are "invariably" wrong in print. But use them with care—write exactly what you mean.

## Accurate Spelling

I've seen how-to books in print that were riddled with spelling mistakes. In one book on automobile tuning, for example, the word "gauge" was misspelled "guage" every one of the hundred or so times it was used!

My reaction to that sort of error is something like this: "I'm looking for guidance on something that I know very little about, in this case automobile tuning. But on the subject of spelling, which I do know about, the author shows himself ignorant and careless. Obviously, he has never carefully read any other book on the subject. Obviously he has never even taken a close look at the instrument he keeps talking about, the box it came in, the instruction leaflet that accompanied it, or its listing in the manufacturer's catalog. I don't feel I can trust him."

"Overcritical," you say?

I don't think so. We regularly judge other people and things by significant details. Suppose at a restaurant you notice that the menu is greasy, the tablecloth is ketchup-stained, and the waiter's hands are dirty. Those details have scant logical connection with the quality of food that may be cooking in the kitchen. All the same, you'll probably walk out without ordering.

The book I mentioned seemed to have been published by the author himself, or by some small printer. A major publisher would not have let such gross spelling errors get into print.

Yet an author's bad spelling may sometimes impair his chances of acceptance by a big publisher. Suppose a publisher receives two or three submissions on the same subject at the same time. (It's not unusual; sometimes a certain subject seems to be "in the air," and several writers rush to deal with it.) Sloppy, inaccurate spelling in one submission may make an editor doubt that author's accuracy in other matters, too.

---

### Exercise 12:9

Check your script for spelling mistakes.

---

# Be Concise

This is no place to be expounding the basic rules of sentence structure and grammar, since all those may be found in other books. What I mean by "style" in this chapter is the development of a sense of what is good, what is better, what might be *best*, to express in words a particular piece of instruction in a way that will most effectively convey information to the reader.

In this particular specialized type of writing that we have here under discussion, one can scarcely overrate the importance of taking care to exercise the most stringent economy in the use of our basic raw material—namely of *words*, just as, in making furniture, one does not waste wood, or in making jewelry one does not waste gold.

It has sometimes been suggested—and it may quite possibly be true—that the oft-repeated habit of never using one word where two, three, or more can be substituted springs from the practice, formerly quite common and still, unfortunately, not yet quite abandoned, of publishers' remunerating writers by the word. The more words such writers produced, obviously, the more lucrative would be their labors; so, in such circumstances, it is scarcely surprising that the temptation toward excessive and undue verbosity would prove well-nigh irresistible!

What's to be learned from that three-paragraph example of verbosity?

(a) Eliminate unnecessary material. The first sentence is an example of "pointing out the hole in the carpet"—telling the reader what you are *not* going to tell him. So cut it out.

The second sentence merely says in other words what has already been said in the first paragraph of this chapter. So cut it out.

The entire third paragraph is irrelevant to this book; in no way does it help readers to write better how-to material. So cut it out.

The last 19 words of paragraph 2 are superfluous. Similes can serve a purpose in clarifying something that, stated by itself, is obscure. But the theme of this paragraph—eliminate unnecessary material—is perfectly clear by itself.

Similarly, in a book on how to make wooden furniture it would be irrelevant to write a long lamentation on the shrinkage of our virgin forests, the need for conservation, new reforestation policies, etc. It's all true and worthy; but it's irrelevant to the furniture book. If you want to write about it, make it into a magazine article!

(b) In writing the essential material, don't waste words. Keep checking your script for ways to say things more briefly.

"In this particular specialized type of writing that we have here under discussion . . ." should be replaced by "In how-to writing . . ." No other type of writing is under discussion in this book!

(c) Be sparing with adjectives and adverbs. For example, the noun "economy" carries the desired meaning without "most stringent." "Material" needs only "raw" and can do without "basic."

In that superfluous third paragraph, " . . . it may be true . . ."

would serve just as well as " . . . it may quite possibly be true . . . "
A habit is by definition an oft-repeated action; so "oft-repeated" is
superfluous. "Verbosity" means the use of an excessive number of
words, so "excessive and undue" is not needed.

In drafting and rewriting, keep looking for superfluous adjectives
and adverbs; your script will be better without them.

So let's see how the "be concise" principle could apply to rewriting our horrible example.

"In how-to writing, be economical with your raw material—
words."

That's 11 words instead of 218.

## But Not Too Concise

Many books—novels, histories, biographies, for example—depend
for their effect on being read through in order from start to finish. A
successful how-to book will be used often for reference; various sections will be consulted separately. Each section must therefore be
fairly complete in itself to spare the reader too much turning back
and forth.

For example, suppose in a cookbook I offer this recipe for Uncle
Raymond's Special Birthday Seedcake:

"To twice the Regular Seedcake recipe (see page 17), add the General Purpose Birthday Fruit Mixture (see page 42); mix as for the
Homecoming Nut Cake (see page 30) and bake one quarter again as
long as the Golden Wedding Cake (see page 55)."

That sort of thing sets the reader turning back and forth, trying to
consult four pages and do mental arithmetic at the same time. It may
be a well-meant effort to save wordage and thus squeeze more recipes into the book, but the result is that many of the recipes will not
be used at all.

The same principle would apply to many kinds of instructive material—diet charts, physical exercises, schedules for seed planting in
specific climates, etc. The general rule is that each instructional item
should be as close to complete as possible. Imagine that your reader
is going to tear that item out of the book and pin it up over the workbench, the stove, the desk, or wherever it's going to be applied.

## The Benefits

Concise, close-packed writing is easier for the reader to grasp and to
apply than a verbose, sloppy style. Moreover, the wordage saved by
a concise style lets you pack into your article or book a maximum of
the real meat and potatoes of your subject. You can give more practical instructions, more experiments, recipes, exercises, diagrams,
photos, maps, etc., when no space is wasted on needless words.

**Exercise 12:10**

"The most valuable of talents is that of never using two words when one will do," said Thomas Jefferson. Cultivate that talent. Check your script for wordy passages; rewrite any such passages in a more concise style.

# Be Specific

"After the plants are set in place, don't be overgenerous with your first few waterings of them. You don't want the soil to get too moist."

The author, no doubt, understands what he means, but he has not conveyed it to the reader. It would be better to prescribe so many cups, pints, liters, or gallons of water, every fourth, fifth, or sixth day—whatever is required; and he should give visual and tactile tests that will unmistakably determine whether the soil is too moist or too dry.

"Sand until the table is smooth enough for varnishing." That's not specific enough. Tell the reader what grades of sandpaper to use, and how to decide when the wood is smooth enough.

Seek always the specific word rather than the vague one. Beware of vague verbs such as "make," "fix," "fasten," "join," "produce." Instead of "firmly fix" say "nail," "screw," "rivet," "glue," "weld," or whatever is appropriate.

Beware of vague quantities: "some," "a few," "a lot," "not many," "an adequate amount," etc. Give specific numbers, weights, measures, temperatures, pressures, lengths, breadths, etc. In Chapter 2, I did not say, "Leave ample margins around the pages of your script." I specified the width of margins required.

Beware of vague times: "early," "halfway through," "soon after," "sometime," and so on. Whenever possible, specify seconds, minutes, hours, days, weeks, months, or years.

"It's best not to hurry the rewriting process unduly," I might say. But that is so vague as to have no practical value. More specific would be, "Lay your script aside overnight and try rewriting it the next morning."

I saw a newspaper gardening column about over-winter care of gladiolus corms. It said that, when you lift the full-size corms in fall, you may find some new cormlets attached to them. The columnist told his readers to detach and save "any good-sized cormlets."

Then, obviously, he realized that to many readers "good-sized" would mean nothing, so he explained that any cormlets "the size of a pea or larger" were big enough to be saved.

Later in the same column, though, he recommended storing the corms in a cool place. That's vague; my idea of "cool" might be your idea of "warm."

**Exercise 12:11**

Check your script for imprecise terms or descriptions. Replace them with specific ones.

## Be Consistent

How-to writing commonly contains an assortment of abbreviations, symbols, and technical terms. You will have to judge which of these your readers are sure to understand and which you should explain to them.

Then aim to be consistent in your use of all those terms and symbols.

For example, in a gardening book, don't give a temperature as 10° C in one place and 50° F elsewhere. Don't express lengths differently in different places—10' 6" here and 10 ft. 6 in. there; or 17 cubic centimeters in one place, 17 cc in another, and 17 ml in a third.

Where there are alternative spellings of any word, choose one and stick to it throughout.

In book writing, where the work may be spread over many months, it is particularly easy to violate this rule of consistency. But consistency does make things easier for readers. Moreover, it makes the index easier for you to compile and more helpful for the reader to consult.

**Exercise 12:12**

Check your script for consistency in the use of abbreviations, technical terms, symbols, etc.

## Be Interesting

Good how-to writing is not just a listing of materials and procedures; it aims to make, and keep, the reader interested. There are techniques for arousing and sustaining interest. Playwrights use them; fiction writers use them; and nonfiction writers can very well use them, too.

**1. Create suspense!**  A novelist can create suspense on the large scale—set the reader wondering whether or not, two hundred pages later, the handsome potter is going to marry the beautiful weaver.

But you can do it on a small scale, by creating suspense within sentences and paragraphs. The reader will not be conscious of what you are doing, but he will feel the effect all the same. He will feel that your script is interesting; he will want to read on.

"The way in which your computer is programmed determines its efficiency and utility." That is a valid statement; but it can be made in a more interesting way.

"The efficiency and utility of your computer depend on how it is programmed."

The first version gives the answer before it states the problem. The second version sets a problem—"What will make my computer efficient and useful?"—and then gives the solution. This structure raises a flicker of curiosity in the reader's mind.

To use suspense effectively in sentences or paragraphs:

(a) Promptly announce a subject of interest to the reader. The "throat-clearing" openings I mentioned earlier do not announce the subject soon enough.

(b) Make the reader want to know, or promise to tell him, something about the subject; arouse his curiosity. Sometimes the mere mention of the subject will serve. In a book for writers the sentence opening, "Better sales prospects for your scripts . . ." will surely arouse interest.

Sometimes you may have to create curiosity by something you say about the subject: "And now abideth faith, hope, charity, these three; but the greatest of these . . ."

Here curiosity is aroused; the reader wants to know *which* is the greatest.

(c) Satisfy the reader's curiosity—relieve the suspense—*at the end* of the sentence or paragraph. " . . . but the greatest of these is charity." There is suspense created and resolved within seven words.

Thomas Edison said "Genius is 1 percent inspiration and 99 percent perspiration."

Here the most surprising part of the formula is kept to the end. True, it is a minor surprise to hear that only 1 percent inspiration is required; we run-of-the mill folks had thought that genius was all inspiration. Yet that "1 percent inspiration" phrase immediately arouses a mental question (the mind calculates very fast!): "Then what makes up the rest of genius?" The answer comes—slap!—in the last four words.

(d) I said above, "Relieve the suspense *at the end*. . . ." Once the suspense is relieved, don't tail off with weaker material.

Earlier in this chapter I wrote, "A paragraph—it may consist of one sentence or several sentences—conveys a major unit of the subject matter." That sentence *ends* with the main statement about paragraphs that I wanted to make at that time.

An alternative version might have been: "A paragraph conveys a major unit of the subject matter. It may consist of one sentence, or several sentences." Here, the main statement about paragraphs is made in the first sentence; the second sentence is less important, less interesting.

The effect seems slight? Indeed it is, in one sentence, or one paragraph. But, if repeated often enough, weak endings raise in the reader's mind a feeling of boredom and disappointment.

**2. Create variety.**  I have already mentioned the advantages of varying sentence and paragraph lengths as a means of adding interest to the work. Vary your sentence structure, too. Despite all that I have just said about the value of suspense, I would certainly not recommend trying to create suspense within every sentence. That would be like sprinkling pepper on every item of the menu.

**3. Involve your readers.**  Some writers think it is more "literary" to use an impersonal style. For example, "care must be taken, when using carbon paper, that the carbon side is not in fact pressing against the back of the top sheet."

Or, "For the would-be writer, a valuable asset would be fast, accurate typing. It is not uncommon to see potential literary careers bog down on failure to achieve this. A lot of typing is necessary as scripts are pushed through numerous rewrites."

In this style, sentence subjects, as far as possible, are impersonal—"care," "asset," "it," "a lot." The writer using this sort of style seems to be holding himself, and his subject matter, at a distance from his readers.

Another device is the use of impersonalities such as "Better results ensue, in the judgment of this writer, when one adopts a more direct, person-to-person style in addressing one's readers." Personal pronouns—"I," "you," "me," "we"—and personal adjectives—"my," "your," "our"—are avoided.

I think that such stylistic mannerisms are out of date, especially in what ought to be the practical, no-nonsense forms of the how-to book and article.

So reveal yourself unashamedly in your writing, with the words "I," "me," and "my"; hook the reader into the doing, experimenting, learning procedures with "you" and "your."

---

**Exercise 12:13**

Check your script for interest. A good test is to read it aloud. Tape-record your reading and play it back to hear what it sounds like. Better still, get someone else, who is not already familiar with the script, to read it aloud while you listen.

This test will show up passages that are ponderous, convoluted, or obscure. When it does, you know just where to begin rewriting.

---

## The Ben Franklin Exercise

Ben Franklin used this method to teach himself to write well:

(a) Find a piece of good published writing—the same kind of work you want to do—somewhere from 250 to 1,000 words. Make a summary of it in about 10 percent of the original length.

(b) Put the summary aside for a few days.

(c) From your summary, and without looking at the original piece, write a script the same length as the original.

(d) Compare your version with the original; carefully analyze all the differences you find. If yours is inferior, find out why.

(e) Put the summary away again for a few days.

(f) Repeat stages (c) and (d).

In this way, you are getting free writing lessons from the author of the original script. Keep up this procedure with different authors and different script samples relevant to your writing plans.

---

### Exercise 12:14

Choose five samples from the Exemplary Dozen and repeat the Ben Franklin exercise with them.

---

## Summary

Good style is important for success.
Good style: clear, concise, accurate, interesting.
Every statement must be clear immediately.
Build an adequate vocabulary.
Keep average sentence length around 15 words.
Keep average paragraph length 50 words or less.
Reveal the sentence topic without delay.
Avoid weak sentence openings.
Be generous with punctuation marks.
Check titles and headings for clarity.
Avoid extravagant statements.
Spell accurately.
Write concisely, but not to the point of being obscure.
Use specific words, not vague ones.
Be consistent in using terms and symbols.
Suspense and variety stimulate interest.
Avoid the impersonal style.

# 13

# Illustrations

 Your planning and research have told you approximately how many and what kinds of illustrations are needed for your book. You may have sent a few samples to the publisher with your proposal. Maybe the publisher has made some suggestions and you have had some negotiations over the actual number of illustrations and which kind should be used where. Eventually those questions are settled.

## Who Does It?

It is often a major problem to decide who shall do the illustrations.

### You?

Many writers would like to illustrate their own books. If you can do it, that will be the most convenient arrangement. It may save you some trouble and money, and it will give you extra credit.

But are you really good enough? Are you already selling photographs and/or artwork for publication? If not, starting on an illustrated book would be like the average Sunday jogger trying to compete in the Olympic Games. Amateurish illustrations sent to a publisher with a proposal will tend to discredit you.

I breakfasted with a publisher the other day. He spent twenty minutes fuming about an author who had just submitted a first-rate how-to script, illustrated with his own third-rate photographs. The publisher would like to buy the script, and get a whole new set of good photos. But "No!" said the author. "*My* photos or no deal!"

So it is probably going to be no deal.

*Good* illustrations, the publisher told me, could quadruple the total sales of a book like that. He is not going to risk his money, and his reputation, on a product that he knows is visually inferior to competing books.

If, though inexperienced, you are determined to try self-illustrating, don't wait till it's time to send out proposals to publishers. Start far ahead—one year, two years, or more—and begin taking adult education courses in commercial photography, commercial art, or both, according to what you need.

Select your courses carefully. Explain to the instructors exactly what you are aiming to do; get them, if need be, to set you special projects, different from the rest of the class.

### Your Collaborator?

Suppose you have a collaborator you know is fully capable of taking photographs and/or drawing diagrams for the book. By all means, let him do it. Agree in advance and see that his share of the book's earnings compensates him for his skill, work, and expenses in doing the illustrations.

But what if the collaborator does *not* have the necessary skill, yet wants to do the illustrations? Or what if he presses to have the work done by some friend or relative who is obviously not good enough?

This is a ticklish situation. You can scarcely come flat out and say that the collaborator, or his daughter, is a bad photographer or artist.

Still, exercising your best mixture of diplomacy and firmness, you must try to talk the collaborator into using a qualified illustrator.

If an expert refuses to yield on this point, he is probably not the collaborator you want. You'd be well advised to abandon the project, at the start, and look for someone else to work with.

### Freelance Illustrators

If you cannot get first-class illustrations from someone within the self-collaborator-family-friend complex, then your best bet is to find some freelance professional artist and/or photographer. These people are usually easy to work with. They are masters of their specialties. They have the required equipment and supplies right at hand. Because of their technical experience, they may offer suggestions that will yield better illustrations than you could have contrived by yourself. The good professional feels that his reputation is always at stake; as he works today, he is thinking of future work opportunities and trying to build a roster of satisfied customers.

Where do you find these capable professionals? It may take a little searching to get the right one or ones. That's another argument for moving ahead with the illustrations as early as possible instead of waiting till the script is finished, or nearly finished.

## Choosing the Right One

Personal recommendation is the best way. Try to find other writers who have used local illustrators, and see what they say of the various people, their abilities, and their temperaments. If you can't get a personal recommendation, you will have to use your own judgment in selecting a photographer and/or artist. Here are a few tips:

(a) Start early. It is not too soon to start the search while you are drawing up the proposal for your book. Study the work of local commercial photographers and artists in locally produced magazines. Try to judge which of them you like. Particularly look for the exact kind or something near the kind of illustrations you will need for your book. Look in the Yellow Pages under "Artists-Commercial" and "Photographers-Commercial."

(b) Before making any phone calls, draw up a short written outline of what the project is and what illustrations will be required. Here's an imaginary example:

> *How to Tap the Clothespin Resource:* an instruction book for making many articles—puppets, doll house furniture, chessmen, various other games and puzzles, miniature animals, birds, and fishes, mobiles, wall ornaments, etc., from clothespins, using just glue, wire, and a few simple tools.
>
> Illustrations required: 44 b&w photos of partly finished and finished articles, some showing hands and tools at work. One should be a waist-up shot of the craftsman to show his face.

This outline will help you hold a quick, coherent phone talk, to see whether this or that photographer or artist is interested.

(c) Make appointments with those you like on the phone to visit their studios and see some of their work. When you arrive, give them a copy of your written outline. There are some photographers and artists, of wide experience, who have never done book illustration work. If that is the case, explain the procedure of book writing and selling. It would be helpful to show one or two how-to books of the same kind as your proposed book to demonstrate exactly what's required.

At first you will probably need just a few sample illustrations to go along with your proposal. Those will show an editor the sort of illustrations you mean to use and will also show the competence of the photographer or artist you have chosen.

Emphasize that, at this pre-proposal stage, you cannot definitely offer much; you don't even know if the book will find a publisher.

Spend some time in conversation with a likely candidate to see if this is the sort of person you can comfortably work with.

Maybe a photographer will take a gamble and supply a few sample photos without immediate payment, with the understanding that, if you sell the book, you will use him for the whole job. But I wouldn't bank on that; more likely you will have to pay for any samples you want.

### The Post-Contract Stage

Once you have sold your book to a publisher, you will know what illustrations are needed and when. You will then be in a stronger position to negotiate with the photographer and artist you have chosen. Make a written agreement before the main work of illustration begins.

There are various possible ways of paying for illustrations:

(a) Flat fee. One lump sum is paid for doing the whole job, perhaps half in advance and the rest on completion.

(b) Payment by the hour. There may be advantages or disadvantages to this scheme, depending on the honesty and competence of the illustrator.

(c) Part payment in cash now, and a share (to be negotiated) in the book's eventual earnings as they come in.

(d) No advance payment. Illustrator's earnings consist entirely of a share of the book's earnings.

There's wide scope for negotiation. Your photographer or artist may be less interested in the money than in the prestige of working on a book and the exposure his work will get all over the continent, and maybe abroad, too.

You will also have to negotiate for rights to the illustrations. Many professional photographers prefer to sell only the rights for certain specific uses of their photographs, while retaining ownership themselves. With black-and-white photos, the photographer usually keeps the negatives and sells only prints. Color transparencies are usually handed over, and often never seen again by the photographer who made them. Yet some photographers will demand the return of transparencies, with a penalty for failure. After the photographs have been published in the book, the photographer then retains the right to sell them again, for other uses, and/or in other parts of the world.

Book rights and first North American serial rights are the terms commonly used for book and magazine illustrations, respectively.

But different publishers have different policies. Some want only the limited rights mentioned above; others prefer to buy *all rights*. That means that the photographer or artist is paid one fee and continues to get credit for his work, but has no control over what future use may be made of it. (Just like the manufacturer who sells you a typewriter.)

Find out from the publisher just what rights will be needed in order to cover all intended uses of your book. Then let that be made clear in your written agreement with a photographer or artist.

Here is a rough draft agreement:

## AGREEMENT

It is hereby agreed that _____ (hereafter referred to as The Author) is to engage _____ (hereafter referred to as The Photographer) to produce photographic illustrations for the book _____ [Title]

The Photographer will supply, in form suitable for reproduction, all photographs necessary for the book, including any retakes or reprints that may be required by The Author or by the publisher. The number of photographs is estimated at approximately _____ black and white, and _____ color.

[Add a paragraph here specifying whatever has been negotiated concerning ownership of rights to the photographs including the rights author and publisher have to use the photographs, in publications or otherwise, and handling of photographs after publication.]

The Author will pay The Photographer a fee of _____. The manner and times of payment shall be as follows. [Set out the terms you have negotiated.]

It is agreed that The Photographer shall receive full credit for his work in the published book, this credit to be in a style and form approved by the publisher.

It is agreed that The Author shall supply The Photographer with one free copy of the book as soon as may be convenient after copies are received from the publisher.

_____ (Author)    (date)_____
_____ (Photographer)    (date)_____

## Illustrations, Useful and Useless

So your book is to be illustrated and you have decided who will do the work. Now comes another problem—exactly what illustrations to have, and how to present them. The wrong subjects for illustration, or the right subjects poorly presented, will simply waste money without enhancing the value of your book for the reader.

## What Is It?

I'm looking at a book on the maintenance and repair of bicycles. It is apparently aimed at complete beginners, because it gives instructions on how to tighten a nut with a wrench and it explains the purpose of a derailleur gear. Nothing wrong with that! Many how-to books are written for beginners.

This book is illustrated with photographs. Some of them are printed right beside the particular instructions that they illustrate. But many are printed in blocks of four, six, and eight pages, bearing no text; and none of the photos has a caption!

I, with twenty-five years' cycling experience, cannot figure out what some of those photos are supposed to show! That sort of thing is no good to the reader; the photographer's skill, time, and work have gone for nothing.

Every illustration should be *instantly identifiable* as showing or explaining something that the reader needs to know. The image is not enough; there must also be an accurate caption adjacent to the illustration.

Also, to get the best value from each illustration, it's advisable to *direct the reader's attention to it*, when you want him to look. (The aforementioned bicycle book never did that; the reader was left to guess at what features of the text were and were not illustrated.)

You may want to refer to some illustrations several times. You should not have to write each time "See the diagram showing the three possible placements of the thingamajig on the whatchamacall-it." So, for convenience, give each illustration a *number*. Then you can simply say "See Figure____"—concise and unmistakable.

Sounds obvious? Nevertheless, some writers and publishers have not discovered it.

It's important that each caption you write be clearly identified with its own illustration, so that there are no mix-ups in the printing process. (That could happen with photos that look pretty much alike—for example, several closely related varieties of roses, or several slightly different steps of some craft process.)

Here's how to reduce the risk:

(a) With big photo prints or diagrams, *don't* write or type your caption or notes on the back. The danger is that the impression of pen, or machine may show through. Even if you don't notice it, the printer's camera may pick it up.

You can type the caption on a sheet or half sheet of paper, and attach it to the bottom of the print or diagram with two strips of tape, applied like hinges—stuck on the *back!* For mailing, fold the sheet that bears the caption up over the face of your illustration.

Or you can lightly write an identification number on the back of the illustration with a felt pen, which does not exert enough pressure to show through, or very lightly with a soft lead pencil. You can also write the number on self-sticking labels. The number refers to a separate list, on which you type your captions. For example, on the back of a photo you would write 8:3, if it's the third illustration of Chapter 8. On the list of captions goes:

---

Figure 8:3. Third stage of the Alchemy process: mixing powdered dross with Philosopher's Stone.

---

(b) Transparencies (35mm) are too small for attached captions. With these, use the number-and-list method—the number goes on the cardboard mount.

## Show Dimensions

I have been looking at a book on general woodworking. This, like the bicycle maintenance book, is aimed at complete beginners. It tells, in considerable detail, how to drive a nail! It is, in general, well illustrated. For example, there is a set of *sixteen* diagrams showing how to mark out and cut the common dovetail joint. Other techniques are described with the same degree of care.

After covering the preliminaries, the author leads his readers on to make some simple pieces of furniture, beginning with a stool and table. Here he provides plans, beautifully drawn except for one defect—no dimensions are included. (Nor are any dimensions given in the text.) No doubt the author could rattle off those dimensions from memory—he is a handicrafts teacher of many years' experience. But those beginner-readers don't know them; the dimensions must be shown!

There should, in fact, be something in every how-to illustration or caption to show—even roughly—the size of the object. In a how-to magazine for backyard gardeners I saw a photo of what was said to be an exceptionally large sunflower, grown by a reader. But the flower head was shown against an ill-defined dark background, with nothing to tell what size it actually was. So the effect of the illustration was lost. The grower's face in the same picture would have shown the scale.

In how-to photography you can often show a hand, a hammer, a screwdriver, a paintbrush, a ladder, a table, or some such object the size of which is instantly recognizable. When that's not practicable, you may be able to put a ruler into the photo somewhere close to the object.

## Be Accurate

In another how-to-build-furniture book, also aimed at beginners, I saw many diagrams showing how to cut out the parts of chairs, tables, bunk beds, bookcases, sofas, and such things. Dimensions were indicated; so far so good. Unfortunately, the diagrams were *not drawn to scale,* so when the reader marked out his wood the pieces would look different from those in the diagrams—some more square, some more oblong, some longer or shorter in relation to the pieces that were supposed to fit with them. That might not bother an experienced woodworker, but it would be disconcerting to a beginner!

That same book also gave perspective sketches of what the various projects should look like when finished. But any reader who took those sketches as honest representations of what he might produce was in for a severe disappointment.

One sketch showed a massive, long, low table of thick timber, such as one might expect to see in the refectory of some castle. Yet anyone who followed the instructions would actually get a shoddy-looking plywood thing resembling a packing case with two of the sides knocked out!

It's not good to leave the reader feeling swindled! That discredits the author, the artist, and the publisher.

### Placement of Illustrations

Illustrations are most effective when the visual image accompanies a verbal idea. That is how, preferably, we are introduced to new people—the new name is given verbally, and simultaneously the new face is presented to the eyesight. That is how we absorb information from those powerful media, film and television.

The ideal arrangement for book illustrations is to have each one on the same page with, or facing, the text to which it refers. Then the reader can make frequent, instantaneous shifts of attention from words to image.

Illustrations are often separated from the passages of text to which they refer, forcing the reader to turn forward and backward, from words to picture. At the very least it is annoying. It's bad enough when the turn is only one or two pages; if the illustration and text are dozens or scores of pages apart, the time lost and the mental distraction of page shuffling seriously impair the value of the illustration.

Sometimes insuperable technical problems demand such a separation. For example, suppose that just a few photographs are called for in a book, in which most of the illustrations are line drawings printed on ordinary text paper. Then it may be necessary to bunch all those photographs together, on a few pages of special paper, somewhere in the middle of the book.

That's not quite what you, as author, would have liked; but you may have to put up with it. Then be prepared to write—or rewrite—your script so that the reader does not have to keep referring to photographs in other parts of the book. Prepare to give him, instead, a diagram that can be printed right along with the text, where it does the most good.

I have before me a beginners' book on taking better photographs. It contains about eighty black-and-white photos and four diagrams scattered through the book, each close to its relevant text. It has two full-page and four half-page color photos printed on four adjacent pages. Two of these illustrate principles of composition; one shows the aesthetic effect of a striking color contrast; one demonstrates how to photograph little children; the others show the uses of tele-photo lenses and polarizing filters. Since none of these adjoins the text to which it refers, the author has given them long, *detailed captions,* to be sure that readers get the point of each one!

That's the best thing to do under the circumstances. Too bad that the author of the previously mentioned bicycle repair book did not think of it!

## Scheduling the Work

After the contract is signed, I would recommend going ahead with the illustrations as you write the text. For one of my early books I did it the other way; I waited till the text was complete and fully revised before starting to assemble the diagrams and photos it required.

That task involved dealing with a photographer and an artist as well as with my text collaborator. I had never imagined such delays and difficulties could occur in an apparently simple project! Each of us four was competent in his own field; but we suffered from misunderstood phone conversations, delays caused by winter weather, several complete stoppages of work because of sickness, and a sudden local shortage of photo film resulting from a labor dispute. The overall responsibility was mine, and the publisher—quite rightly—kept bugging me about when I was going to deliver the goods.

The trouble would have been averted if I had planned for, and insisted upon, what I'm now recommending—get the illustrative work done piecemeal, as each chapter is brought into fairly good shape. Thus you enjoy the satisfaction of having the entire project—words and pictures—moving ahead together. That satisfaction will be shared by the editor, whose job it is to keep tabs on the progress of the work.

## Supervision

If anybody but yourself is doing the illustrations, you should supervise the work closely and continuously. Some photographers, artists, and collaborators have a startlingly casual attitude toward the job. They will, if they get the chance, illustrate various things that they think look good—things that particularly show off their special talents—rather than the things that you have described in the text! The discovery of a batch of such misguided work, near the deadline, will give you a severe shock.

The remedy? Personally supervise every session of photography. You won't want to sit watching an artist all the time he is drawing; but at least inspect and check the work often, in small batches, so you can see that he is keeping on track.

Remember, you are responsible to the publisher for the whole project—text and illustrations; so you must take and keep control of these sometimes eccentric people.

## Format

Publishers differ in their preferences as to format of illustrations. For photographs, 8x10-inch (20x25-cm) glossies for black and white and 35mm transparencies for color are the most common sizes; but they are by no means universally accepted. Book publishers' individual preferences are listed in *Photographer's Market*, and you'd be wise to consult that source before you submit.

A good idea is to take a mix of horizontal and vertical photos of your chosen subjects. That gives an editor more scope for arranging the material on the pages of the book.

Diagrams are commonly drawn on 8x10-inch (20x25-cm) sheets.

## Copyright

For some kinds of subjects—arts and crafts, for example—you may be able to get all the illustrations you need from your own or your collaborator's work. For others—remodeling houses, restoring antiques, landscape gardening, boat building, for example—you may want to photograph other people's work.

It's best to begin the search for suitable photos as soon as you start planning the book. For some subjects, you may be able to get good photographs from government departments, trade associations, magazines, and stock photo houses. (See "Photographs—Stock" in the Yellow Pages of your phone book, or consult *Literary Market Place* for stock photo agencies.)

To avoid risk of copyright problems, particularly with art and craft works from outside sources, it's a good precaution to get a written release from the person who made the object or who owns the rights to the photo. Here's an appropriate wording:

RELEASE
For value received, I hereby assign to author _____ , and publishers designated by the author, book rights to the photo-

graphs listed below, for use as illustrations in the book provisionally titled _____ .
[Here list the photos covered by the release.]
_____ (Signature)        (Date) _____
_____ (Author)           (Date) _____

The release does not have to specify the "value received." Maybe it has been a meal, a drink, or just the artist's personal satisfaction at having his work thus publicized. But, if you do make any cash payment, get a separate receipt for it.

**Exercise 13:1**

In the Exemplary Dozen, analyze illustrations.

(a) Which, if any, of the illustrations do you think might have been omitted?

(b) Can you think of any other illustrations that should have been included?

(c) Can you find examples of illustrations whose value is lessened, or destroyed, because of some omission (e.g., missing dimensions)?

(d) Can you see any instances where the purpose would have been better served by another type of illustration—a diagram instead of a photo, or vice versa; an exploded diagram instead of an all-in-one diagram, etc?

(e) Examine the use of color in illustrations. Where is it necessary and instructive? Where is it only ornamental?

(f) Do you see any illustrations that are badly misplaced? If so, can you figure out where they should preferably be located?

(g) Analyze the captions. How well do they help you understand what the illustrations are meant to tell the reader?

(h) If you find some bad captions, try rewriting them to make them more effective.

(i) How effective is the text-to-illustration reference? Does the author promptly show how and where he is offering illustration for your guidance?

## Summary

Amateurish illustrations impair selling prospects.
Beware of unskilled collaborators or friends.
In dealing with professional illustrators, be businesslike.
Every illustration must be promptly identifiable.
Refer unmistakably from text to illustrations.

Show the dimensions of objects illustrated.
Make all illustrations accurate and honest.
Write to obtain maximum value from illustrations.
Start illustrating as early as possible.
Personally supervise illustrative work.
Check copyright of bought illustrations.
Observe other writers' good and bad use of illustrations.

# 14

# Promotion

 The day you mail the book index to your publisher marks the end of your writing work on the project. But you have more work to do in helping to sell the book.

So far only you, and maybe a few of your family and friends, plus a few people at the publisher's office, are aware of the book's existence. The people who buy books do not know that you are writing, or have written, a book.

So, before your book is ready to go on sale, something must be done to remedy that ignorance. The ideal is to tell many thousands of people about the book, and get them interested enough in it to pay money for it. That process of promoting the sales of the book is the subject of this chapter.

Some authors, in some branches of writing, take a highfalutin attitude toward this process. But we how-to writers are more practical, I hope. We like to find out what makes things tick; we like to experiment in pulling levers and turning wheels ourselves.

So here are some ways in which an author can help promote his writing and himself, earn more money, and in the process, have a bit of pleasure.

## Browsers, Ahoy!

A how-to book is likely to carry several short, emphatic items that tell what the book is about, and what it can do for a reader. For example, I have before me a paperback edition of a bestselling physical fitness book.

(a) On the front cover is a 21-word excerpt from the text, chosen to reinforce the effect of the title.

(b) On the first page is a punchy nine-point list—about 120 words—of major benefits to be obtained from following the author's fitness system.

(c) On the back cover is a 150-word summary of the system.

In a hardback book, similar material will probably be placed on the inside flaps and back of the jacket.

The purpose of such material is to make a quick, strong appeal to potential purchasers who may pick up the book in a store. They are used to this kind of appeal; they habitually look for it and may be influenced by it to glance at the table of contents, to look at a few pages in the body of the book, and perhaps to buy it.

This material is usually written by someone at the publisher's office. Still, you may be asked to contribute some ideas or notes for it.

---

**Exercise 14:1**

Study the promotional material in the Exemplary Dozen.

(a) How accurate, and how interesting, are the general summaries?

(b) How attractive are any such lists of benefits?

---

**Exercise 14:2**

You have drafted an outline for your book. Now reduce that to 150 words, styled so as to arouse interest and curiosity—and make the browser look further into the book.

(a) Make a list of a few (not more than ten) benefits that a reader might get from the book. Each item should be brief—not more than ten words.

(b) Try to find some short excerpt from the text of your book that sums up the essence of what you are saying.

---

You don't have to wait till the script of a book is finished to do these exercises. You can try your hand at them during pauses in the writing of the first draft, or between subsequent rewrites. Exercise 14:2, in particular, will help to sharpen your judgment as to what must be put into the book and what would be better left out.

## Business Cards

In Chapter 11 I mentioned using a business card when appearing for an interview. Every writer who wants to cultivate a professional attitude should have some cards designed and printed.

A card is the quickest way to introduce yourself in business offices, government departments, libraries, and such places. The card inspires confidence. It makes you feel confident because you are showing yourself to be well prepared and efficient. It makes the recipient feel confident that you are a solid citizen who has at least lived in one place long enough to acquire a permanent address.

A card is especially useful when you are meeting people at parties and other social events. When you are standing with a cup of coffee in one hand and a sandwich in the other, it's difficult to write down your name and address. It's much quicker and more businesslike to pass over a card.

Retail stationers, stationery departments of big stores, and some printers can show you samples of designs and typefaces. Choose what you think best expresses your personality.

What's to go on the card?

(a) Your name, preferably in the form that you want to see it used on your published work. For example, my friends call me Ray, but I have always used Raymond for writing because it gives a better balance with my one-syllable surname. I have a middle name, Horace, but I do not use that or its initial. So the name on my scripts and on my card is Raymond Hull.

(b) Your address and telephone number.

(c) You may want to indicate the kind(s) of work you do.

Here are a few examples from cards that I have.

One man simply has "Writer," centered beneath his name.

A woman has:

| |
| --- |
| Writing |
| Photography |
| Public Relations |

Another woman uses

| |
| --- |
| Writer/Photographer |
| Magazines—Newspapers—Publicity |

All these are good. But I have seen cards cluttered up with details about the owner and his career—fifteen or twenty words in small type, plus the name and address. That's too much.

Bear in mind that the card serves primarily to tell people your name and address; and—this is important—it works best if it is legible *at a glance*.

Plan what you want on the card before you go shopping. Then get at least 100 printed for your first order. If you are not likely to be moving soon, order 500 at a time to save money. Then make a point of *always* carrying a few everywhere you go. You never know when you might need one.

## Promotion Leaflets

By advising against cluttering up business cards with too many details of your qualifications and attainments, I certainly do not mean that you should be secretive about such things. There is a better place for them: the personal promotion leaflet.

I have been using such leaflets, regularly updated, for years. At present I have two different ones in print:

### General Promotion

This contains:

(a)  A list of my books in print, the title of each, a brief (ten to forty words) summary of the subject, and the name of the publisher. (N.B. I do not include prices. Book prices may differ from store to store and city to city.)

(b)  A list of my plays in print, each with title, summary, cast requirements, length, and publisher.

(c)  Lecture notice, briefly stating that I am sometimes available for lectures to conventions, clubs, etc.; the name and address of my lecture agent.

This material, single-spaced, occupies both sides of an 8½x11-inch (22x28-cm) sheet of white paper. I believe it's important that such a leaflet not be more than one sheet! As necessary, I omit or abbreviate items to keep the total material within that space limit.

### Writers' Consultation Service

This leaflet lists twenty problems on which I find writers often want advice. It describes my conditions and fees for a two-hour personal consultation on such problems. Then follows my name, address, and phone number. This material fills one side of a standard-size sheet.

### Leaflet Production

In preparing the text for such leaflets, there's no need to be dishonest. But remember the twin purposes—to *inform* and *impress* the recipients.

So don't include material that will not be impressive. Consider what sort of people you are aiming at with those leaflets.

The way I produce the leaflets is to type out a master copy of each one, and then have the required number of copies made by a commercial photocopying firm. I usually get 250 copies done at a time.

### Using Promotion Leaflets

When you have made your leaflets, don't skimp on using them. You can hand over an appropriate leaflet at your first business meeting with someone—a potential collaborator, an editor, a publisher, a photographer. It's the quickest, most effective way to establish your credentials.

You can mail a leaflet as part of a query or proposal, or in response to some inquiry about yourself and your work.

You can hand over a leaflet when you are being interviewed for the press, radio, or TV. Thus, instead of just sitting, waiting to be questioned, you are to some extent directing the course of the interview.

Always remember that it's no use to sit at home, waiting and hoping for someone to discover you and your talents! Plan and produce whatever promotional material is appropriate for you. The slight investment of time and money will be repaid umpteen times over in publicity, in work opportunities, in cash, and in personal satisfaction.

---

### Exercise 14:3

Draft a general promotion leaflet for yourself, using the principles described in this chapter.

---

## Book Reviews

When a new book comes out, the publisher sends copies to newspapers and magazines that are likely to review it. He probably has a good general knowledge of the periodical press, but he may ask you for names of any papers or magazines which, for any reason, might take a particular interest in you and your work.

Try to come up with some suggestions on this; some neighborhood weekly papers, for example, run reviews of locally written books. Maybe your old school, your firm, your church, or some club you belong to has a magazine that would give your book a write-up.

In the next stage, some local reviewer may phone you for information about yourself—over and above what is in the book. It's useful to have a list of autobiographical tidbits ready so that you can rattle them off on request. Don't be led, by the excitement of the moment, into revealing material that you would rather have kept hidden!

## Interviews

After you have published a book, or a noteworthy magazine article, some local journalist may ask you for an interview. For a book, an interview can lead to a longer review or, perhaps, two separate items—the review plus a personality piece.

Have your promotion leaflet ready; also thoroughly refresh your memory on whatever you are going to talk about. (One journalist told me of an author who replied to the first question, "Gosh! It's so long since I wrote that book that I've forgotten what's in it!")

Any interviewer will likely conclude by asking about your future plans. It sounds amateurish to reply, "Er . . . well . . . I don't really know what I'll be writing next. I . . . er . . . kind of wait to see what turns up!"

It's better if you are prepared with some positive-sounding statement. As I note in regard to the "production line" system in Chapter 15, you should always be working on, or planning, several pieces of writing.

An interviewer may bring a camera and want to photograph you. So fix yourself up as you would like the public to see you. Do you have a special work place where you do your writing? Then suggest taking the photo there—author at the desk, author at the typewriter, etc. Take the precaution of having the work place tidy—or untidy—as befits the image you want to project.

## Broadcast Media

Radio and television interviews can be potent means of promoting you and your work. Here are some hints for making broadcast interviews enjoyable and productive:

1. Advance information. Sometimes a radio or TV program will ask you to send them some information about yourself.

(a) Send a copy of the book or article that is the primary subject of the interview (unless they specifically tell you that they already have a copy).

(b) Send copies of promotional leaflets, reviews, or anything that may possibly be relevant.

(c) Send a short autobiographical note; 100 to 150 words should be enough.

Make sure that this material reaches the station in ample time.

2. Just as you did for the living-room interview, refresh your memory on the subject matter.

3. Make notes of some up-to-the-minute items concerning your subject—*new* reactions to the work, or *new* tidbits of information on the subject. Bear in mind that the broadcast media want to offer, and must have, a constant stream of *new* material that the listening and viewing public has not obtained elsewhere.

For example, I gave an interview the other day, for a local radio station, on my thirteen-year-old book, *How to Get What You Want.* I briefly reviewed the general theory of the book, then brought out my up-to-the-minute item:

"I'm still teaching night school courses based on that book. At the end of the last ten-week term one man, long unemployed, had found a job; one woman had lost ten pounds; another woman had lost fifteen pounds; and a third woman had got herself a new boyfriend!"

For a TV interview, choose a few exhibits on your subject, if you have any that are portable—finished pieces of whatever it is that you make, plans or diagrams, tools, equipment, etc. Television interviewers like such material; they put the cameras on the exhibits while they are talking to you about them.

4. You will be told what time to arrive at the studio. Be punctual! Broadcast programs are run strictly by the clock.

5. You meet the person who will interview you. Sometimes this meeting takes place several minutes before the show begins, allowing time for a few pleasantries.

One important point: Don't discuss, with the interviewer or with anyone else, the material you are going to use on the air. If you do you are likely to get, in the middle of your airtime, an awful feeling: "Oh, Lord! I've said this before! I'm repeating myself!" That's very disconcerting; it can even make you dry up altogether.

At some interviews you just meet the interviewer during a sixty-second commercial break; there's only time for a handshake, a quick greeting, and you are on.

6. Microphones. For radio, the mikes are likely to be standing on a desk or table at which you have to sit. For TV, they may use some kind of pin-on or hang-on microphone, or perhaps a microphone on a long, mobile boom. Whatever the setup, you may be asked to do a short test speech so that technicians can adjust the sound apparatus to suit the volume and timbre of your voice.

If you are at a loss and can't think of anything to say, you'll look amateurish. So *be prepared* with something. "Good afternoon. My name is So-and-So. I'm a writer, specializing in how-to material, although I also do a bit of singing, guitar playing, and gambling on the side. I'm here this afternoon to give an interview about such-and-such." Write out some such brief introduction, learn it, and be ready with it. A little speech like this may be enough.

If a longer test is required, someone will tell you. Then a useful trick is to give a description of how you traveled to the studio. "I left my home at such-and-such address, shortly after x o'clock this morning, and walked one and a half blocks to my usual bus stop at the intersection of Umpteenth Avenue and Zillionth Street . . . "etc.

Draw it out; give all the details of the journey. This will sustain you through the longest test. The method has two advantages: (1) Again, it avoids the danger of talking prematurely about your subject. (2) This little demonstration of your ability to rattle away confidently and coherently makes the interviewer and other studio personnel feel more at ease about the coming interview. When they feel at ease, it helps you to feel at ease; and that's just what is needed for a successful interview.

During the test, someone may interrupt you with a request to speak louder or softer, more quickly or more slowly, or (in radio) to speak closer to the microphone. Try to remember these instructions all through the session.

---

### Exercise 14:4

Prepare for a broadcast interview. For this exercise you need a tape recorder and the cooperation of a friend.

The friend opens with "Now, So-and-So, we're going to do a little voice test. Will you speak into this microphone, please?"

You begin your spiel. The friend interrupts you with various requests. "Say that over again, please." "Try making it about 10 percent louder." "Can you slow down somewhat?"

Let the friend be inventive, and come up with various other gimmicks to try and throw you off balance.

Listen to the playback and see how well you obeyed the instructions.

Normally you will not undergo so much fuss in a real interview. The purpose of this exercise is to give you practice in controlling your voice with a microphone stuck in front of your face.

---

7. Head and face control. For radio, keep your head in the position that was approved during the test. No turning or leaning back, except when you are sure you're off the air.

Smile often, even if you must force it. The smile, though unseen by listeners, creates a warmer, richer tone of voice than does a straight face.

For television, keep looking at the interviewer. Don't try to watch the cameras or the studio audience, if there is one. Here, too, smile often; it helps you appear relaxed.

8. If some of your exhibits are being shown, you will see them on a monitor—a TV screen hanging or standing nearby. Speak of an exhibit as it appears on the monitor, because that's the image that the viewer is receiving. E.g., if the monitor shows only one end, or one side of something, talk about the part that is visible. If exhibits come on screen in a different order from what you had planned, keep calm and adapt your remarks accordingly.

9. The conclusion. Don't bother yourself with trying to keep track of time. The interviewer does that; and he knows how to bring an interview gracefully to a close. So simply cooperate with him.

One thing is absolutely taboo—a sudden outburst, right at the end: "Oh, but there's one thing, one very important thing that I simply *have* to mention. The real purpose behind this process that I've been describing is to . . . " and so on.

It will do you no good. The control room can cut you off at the flip of a switch. The result of such an outburst is a bad ending to the interview; you look incompetent and the interviewer regards you as a nuisance. (If he came to your home and threw sand in your typewriter, you would regard *him* as a nuisance, wouldn't you?)

## Good Interviews

I have written at length about being interviewed because it is very important. Some writers take a snooty attitude toward the daily press and the broadcast media, considering journalists and interviewers to be somehow inferior.

Don't kid yourself! Those journalists and broadcast interviewers are all making a full-time living from their skill with words! They are *experts* in their own fields. We freelancers have much to learn from them.

Try to build the reputation of always giving a good interview, for both the newspapers and the airwaves. That reputation will be a precious asset!

## Summary

Promotion helps sell books.

Get, and regularly use, printed business cards.

Design, and regularly use, personal promotion leaflets.

Look for book review opportunities.

Cooperate with reviewers and journalists seeking information.

Prepare well for radio and TV interviews.

Cooperate with studio staff for a smooth session.

# 15

# How to Build a Writing Career

 Sometimes nonwriters say, "Mr. Hull, your life and work must be *so* glamorous. I'd give *anything* to be a writer! Tell me, how should I start?"

I say, "Buy a typewriter and learn to use it."

The usual reply is, "Oh, but that would take time and money!"

No "Open Sesame" instantly admits a nonwriter into the exciting but arduous career of professional or semiprofessional writing.

But there are some steps you can take, if you want to.

## Typing

My suggestion about typing is no joke. I have heard of writers succeeding while using spouses, friends, or paid secretaries to do their typing. The first two procedures put a severe strain on love or friendship; the third is expensive. More important, all three cause severe *waste of time* in the laborious early stages of writing and rewriting.

If you have a lot of lucrative work in hand, you may be able to profit by paying someone to type your final clean copies. You need a little cost analysis to see whether that expense justifies itself.

As for my typewriter recommendation, ". . . learn to use it," I don't suggest that you sit down in front of the newly bought machine and try to learn by the hunt-and-peck system. Get some proper instruction! Go to night school or a commercial school and learn touch typing. Whatever time you spend in acquiring that skill is repaid many times over as you develop your writing career.

## Writing Instruction

Some writers boast of how they struggled for years, and suffered several hundred rejections, before making the first sale. To my mind, that shows a mistaken approach to the art and business of writing.

Architects, lawyers, dancers, singers, boxers, swimmers, surveyors, and diamond drillers—members of all skilled trades and professions—expect to take instruction before they begin to earn money by their work.

But many writers think they learned to write in school, so they need no further instruction.

That schooling is not enough to make you a *writer*, regularly published in books and magazines! Most people who try to become writers with only that basis of knowledge fail repeatedly, become discouraged, and quit. Only the few exceptionally strong-willed— like those I cited above—will persevere till they succeed.

There is an easier, quicker way. Get expert instruction! Courses in nonfiction writing are available everywhere. I think that classroom instruction is best, at least at the start. It gives the closest, quickest contact between teacher and student and it gives you the benefit of stimulating discussion with fellow students.

See what nonfiction writing courses are available from your local adult education service, from university extension departments, colleges, community centers, etc. If they don't already have any such course, suggest that they get one started. (Most of them welcome new ideas.)

Don't be skimpy about taking this instruction. Don't assume that two hours a week for ten or fifteen weeks is going to turn you into an accomplished writer. Take all the relevant courses you can find. Take the same courses over and over again. Do all the writing assignments the instructor sets, and more. Make yourself produce scripts, and have them criticized; that is more valuable than simply sitting and listening to the lectures.

If you absolutely cannot attend any classes, then take correspondence courses. The more you put into such a course in the way of script writing, the more you get out of it in the way of increased knowledge and skill.

Go to writers' conventions; they are regularly held all over the continent. There you can hear lectures from, and talk with, some of the best writers in your chosen field.

Regularly read writers' magazines; buy, and work your way through, books of instruction for writers.

Join a writers' club. If you don't know of one, ask at your public library. If there is no such club near you, form one. Write to the editors of local newspapers, announcing your plan; they may give you some publicity. Pin up notices in library branches, night schools, community centers, churches, supermarkets—anyplace where they might catch the eye of some writer.

Get your club organized and start holding regular meetings; arrange lectures from experienced club members, and from visiting speakers. Form small groups for script reading and mutual criticism.

Continually study and practice to improve your writing skill and speed.

### Keep Learning

Even when you are selling regularly, don't stop learning. However much you know about writing, you can always learn more.

Books, magazines, lectures, clubs, conventions—by whatever means possible, keep on expanding and updating your knowledge. The technical, aesthetic, and business aspects of writing are all subject to change. You should be aware of those changes, and ready to adapt yourself and your work to fit in with them. This is especially true in a field such as how-to writing. A writer who fails to adapt will soon find his work becoming outdated and out of demand; his career will grind to a halt.

### Check the Results

There is one danger in this procedure of nonstop learning: the danger of spending too much time studying and not enough time and effort in *writing*.

"After I've taken one more course, I'll really be ready to start researching my book."

"When the kids are off my hands, I'm planning to go back to the university for a couple of years. Then I'll have the confidence to start writing."

Such are the excuses of the people who just want to *dream* of being writers. Your learning plan must never be used as an excuse for *not writing!*

Seek out whatever writing you can do with the skill and knowledge you have, and *do it*. Then, as you keep learning, keep advancing to bigger, more important, better-paying projects. But certainly, all the way through, *keep writing*. Failure to do that means the time and money you spent on learning has been spent in vain.

---

### Exercise 15:1

Make a list of short writing projects you might undertake today.

## Achieving Fluency

Excessively slow writing is a severe obstacle to career building. Academic presses can afford to wait years, or decades, for scripts; commercial magazine and book publishers cannot!

To make a substantial income, or to build a reputation by your writing, you must be able to turn out the material to a deadline— quickly and reliably.

Here is the best exercise I know for attaining literary fluency.

---

### Exercise 15:2

Choose a word at random—for example, by closing your eyes and sticking a pin into an opened magazine page. (Ignore ifs, ands, buts, etc. Take the nearest word that has some real significance.) Put a sheet of paper into your typewriter. Type that target word as a heading. Then compose at the typewriter, *without stopping*, a full double-spaced page of writing on the subject of that word.

I emphasize *without stopping*. If you can't think what to write next, keep typing the last word over and over again until you can think of how to continue.

Note how long it takes you to complete the full page.

Repeat the exercise daily for several years. You will find that your completion time gradually goes down. You are achieving fluency.

Here are a few notes on the exercise.

(a) Bear in mind that the scripts you produce by this exercise are not final, clean copies; they are rough drafts. Don't feel bad if they contain errors. Remember that the ability to compose *rough drafts* rapidly is a major factor of success in writing! Once you have a full-length rough draft, rewriting is relatively easy.

(b) Here is a useful variant. After some practice with random words, try using as a target word something that you need to write about for your work. See what you can turn out by the same full-page, nonstop technique.

---

### Records

As a check on your fluency, make a fixed practice of recording the number of words you write each day; keep monthly and yearly totals. Watch for changes up or down in your output. Analyze what you have been doing to cause the changes.

For example, as I write the first draft of this book, I am producing about 22,000 words a month. In a few weeks, when I settle down to rewriting, my output will drop. (I count only new material.) But the reason for the drop is good enough.

Then, for a time, while I type the final clean copy, there will be no new production at all. But again, I know the reason—and I have not stopped working!

## Diversify

It's risky to concentrate all your hopes, talents, and work on one magazine or one book publisher. True, that may be a comfortable situation—while it lasts. But a magazine or publishing house may suffer financial difficulties and close down; it may have a change of ownership or editorship, with a resulting change of policy and style.

If some such crisis occurs, you, the faithful freelance writer, may be left stranded. Then you must start in again from scratch to build up your market.

It is easy to slip into some such "single outlet" pattern of writing. But your career will be more soundly based if you avoid it. Even if your present single outlet keeps you fairly busy, make careful, persistent efforts to scout for other outlets too.

## The Production Line

You finish the clean copy of an accepted script, mail it, and celebrate. Then you are struck with the thought, "Oh, Lord! What am I going to write about next?"

There's no need to slip into that quandary. You can arrange to always have at hand an assortment of good subjects for books or articles, and most of them can be at various stages along the road that leads from initial idea to final script. Here's how:

(a) Train yourself to always be on the alert for ideas that suit you and your favored subject or subjects. From conversation, newspapers, books, radio, and television come the ideas. You will also find ideas in stores and museums.

(b) Make a note of each idea as soon as you come across it. (This, by the way, is a sure sign of the real writer: he carries a notebook everywhere, and can often be seen writing in it.) As soon as it is convenient, open a file for each of those new ideas—just one sheet of paper in a manila folder is enough for a start.

(c) Keep gathering material for all your idea files—notes from all sources, newspaper and magazine clippings, etc. Train your mind to always be alert for useful material.

(d) Whenever you have nothing more urgent to write, turn to one of these files; arrange the raw material, make a note of some other material you will need in order to advance the project, and plan to find it. Maybe draft an outline of the project, or write several dozen words in rough form.

By this process, you construct, and fill up, your how-to production line. You keep putting in ideas at one end, as finished articles or books emerge at the other.

And here's a particularly valuable benefit. Sooner or later you reach the point where editors come to you asking for material. Then, with your well-filled production line, you have material to offer. At this stage your how-to writing career is solidly established.

---

**Exercise 15:3**

Open five files for the production line. Write at least 100 words of notes for each.

---

# Literary Agents

Many a beginning writer thinks that all his difficulties would be over if only he could find a literary agent. As a rule, that's not true. A literary agent does not teach beginning writers their trade. His main concern is selling scripts that are good enough to be submitted to a publisher.

Most agents handle only books; few deal in magazine articles. The standard agent's commission is 10 percent of the author's fee. Ten percent of the average article price would not pay an agent for his correspondence, phone calls, and filing costs, let alone his professional skill.

Many literary agents are already so busy with the work of their present clients that they do not want any more.

## When Are You Ready?

You must expect to start your writing career without an agent. Write all you can; sell all you can. Get several successful books to your credit—then you are ready to start querying agents. Study the agents' listings in a writers' directory. Some of them, like publishers, specialize more or less narrowly; so don't waste time querying an agent who does not handle your kind of writing.

## Working with Agents

The agent-author relationship is usually just a gentlemen's agreement—a handshake, but no formal contract. You send a proposal or a script to an agent and he tries to sell it for you. If he can't sell it, he returns it. Or if he thinks some revision would improve its sales prospects, he tells you. You are not forced to obey, but you would probably be wise to do so. The agent's advice is that of an expert whose career is based upon judging what will and will not sell!

An agent may sometimes suggest to you a new book subject, and a style of treatment for it. Here, too, you should give great weight to his expert advice.

## Public Speaking

An enormous asset, financial and social, for any how-to writer is the ability to speak well in public. As a speaker you can help boost the sales of your own published books. But there is much more to it than that. You can build a reputation as a lecturer on your specialty. Good lecture bookings pay hundreds of dollars per hour—that's more than you can earn at the typewriter!

There is also another advantage. The whole business of speaking—going away from home, transmitting ideas and information to a live audience, and learning from them via their questions and comments—makes a stimulating contrast to the usual routine of sitting silently for hours at your desk. There are few feelings more exciting than the speaker-audience relationship in a successful lecture.

The writer's life tends to be solitary and lonely. Every time you go out to speak, you meet new people. Most of these contacts are pleasant and some of them may become valuable for your career. I have met publishers, agents, and other writers in this way. I have been speaking, as a sideline to my writing, for twenty years or so, and I intend to continue.

Now for a warning: Don't assume that, because you have been talking from infancy, you'll have no trouble addressing an audience! Public speaking is an art that must be learned.

People who try to speak in public without knowing how usually annoy or bore their audiences—and they injure their own reputations.

Take some courses in public speaking; many communities offer such courses. If yours does not, write to your adult education authority and ask them to start one. Do a bit of recruiting to find some other people who will come along with you.

Take various public speaking courses from different instructors, if you can find them. If not, keep taking the same courses over and over again, two, three, or more times.

Then practice, by frequent speaking in whatever clubs, societies, political party, church, etc., that you belong to. If you don't belong to any such groups, join a few and make your voice heard; or join one of the widespread public speaking organizations.

When you feel you are getting fluent as a speaker, construct a lecture on your special subject. Plan it in three forms: thirty minutes, forty-five minutes, and one hour, each well rounded and complete in itself. If you feel charitable, try out your lecture free of charge on some groups that you think deserve such a gift.

Then you can begin to *sell* your services. Draft a single-sheet leaflet describing your lecture and yourself. Get a few hundred copies and send them around to organizations that may use speakers at meetings, banquets, conventions, parties, seminars, etc.

In some cities there are lecture agents. Find one in the Yellow Pages of your phone book; see if they will take you as a client. Convention-management firms may also be willing to act as speakers' agents.

If you can't immediately put your finger on any such potential agent, do some research. (You *are* a nonfiction writer, aren't you?) Find some person or firm who will represent you and get bookings for you. Thirty percent of the gross fee is considered a fair commission for lecture agents.

## Teaching

Suppose you are already familiar with some how-to subject and feel you would like to spend considerable time and effort writing on it, perhaps many articles and a book or two.

You will benefit yourself, and your future readers, if you first sharpen your knowledge of it, and enhance your communicative skills, by teaching it part-time in some adult education system. Most such organizations call for no academic qualifications, just a knowledge of the subject and the ability to communicate it.

I taught night school courses in writing for three years before I began to *write* about writing. I taught public speaking for three years before I wrote my book on public speaking. I taught a course called "Dynamic Psychology" for three years before I turned it into the book entitled *How to Get What You Want.*

Teaching offers important advantages for the writer:

(a) Planning the course forces you to analyze your knowledge of the subject. You must break it down into coherent, lesson-size segments; and you must decide what should come first, second, third, etc. In effect, planning a course on your subject automatically provides you with the plan of a book.

(b) The teaching procedure makes you practice explaining, exemplifying, and enriching the subject so that it is comprehensible and interesting. Students' reactions show you precisely where you are succeeding, and where more exemplification, more enrichment, would be welcome.

(c) The feedback from students gives you valuable *new insights* into your subject. Get students talking about their problems, failures, and successes with it; they will give you umpteen ideas that you would not have come up with by yourself. And—particularly valuable—this insight, this research, is *exclusive to you.* No other writer on the subject has it.

(d) The fact that you have *taught* the subject is an impressive addition to your qualifications for writing about it. Quite likely, even the editor of the magazine or book publishing house has not *taught* the subject. He is impressed that you have done so.

(e) After your book is published, you can likely use it as a text in your courses, and make extra money by selling copies to students. Publishers will usually supply you with copies for resale at a discount of 40 percent or thereabouts. (The possibility of such long-continued extra sales might even influence a publisher's initial decision to accept a book.)

## Broadcasting

Some radio stations broadcast how-to material on such subjects as outdoor sports, gardening, handicrafts, cooking, etc.

You will stand the best chance if you write and read your own scripts. That's not as simple as it sounds; you will probably need some instruction and a good deal of practice. Good radio writing differs markedly from writing for the printed page; it should be nearer to a conversational style.

Good radio speaking is very different from platform speaking. On radio, you may be reaching thousands of people simultaneously, yet you are speaking to them separately. You are a guest in their homes; you are a rider in their automobiles. Conventional oratory will sound ridiculous, quite out of place. In voice, too, you must cultivate a conversational manner.

Then there is the question of timing. On the platform, you can fall two minutes short of your allotted time, or run three minutes too long; if you are interesting the audience, it won't matter. But for radio, your timing must be accurate to the second.

So there is a lot of technique behind the casual sound of good radio writing and radio speaking. But lots of other people have mastered it, and so can you. See if your adult education system offers classes in radio broadcasting techniques. Look in the Yellow Pages of your phone book under "Schools—Business," "Schools—Technical and Trade," and such categories. Or phone some radio personality whom you admire and ask for advice on how to get started.

After some training, you could sharpen your skills on one of the volunteer-staffed community radio stations that exist in some places.

When you are ready to go professional with your radio how-to column, it will help if you can find a sponsor—a manufacturer or dealer who sells some product or equipment that is tied in with your subject. For example, a boat dealer for talks on boating, a nursery for gardening talks, a hardware merchant for a home-repair series, etc.

A package like this—the regular short talk and the commercial— would appeal to some radio stations, especially to those that have pretensions to cultural or community service. Good talks, on tape, might then be syndicated with other non-overlapping stations to increase their earnings.

**Television**

For how-to television shows, you must have something visually interesting to offer! It would be ridiculous for me to propose a TV how-to show about writing; no one wants to watch me, for more than a few seconds, tapping the keys of my typewriter.

I know one man who stars in a weekly half-hour cooking show. He has an outgoing personality, and something of a theatrical manner in handling his pots and dishes. He has written a lively, illustrated book describing his methods and recipes; the last I heard, it had sold 160,000 copies and was still going strong.

I know a woman who, for years, gave weekly yoga demonstrations on television and sold umpteen thousand copies of her how-to books.

Much of what I said about radio applies to television: you need training and practice to succeed. But, for good performers with the right subjects, the opportunities are there. And in a few years' time (I write this in 1981), the opportunities will be wider still. Many more TV channels will be available—a hundred or more transmitted clearly, all over the continent, by satellite.

Some of those channels will be allocated to instructional material—dressmaking, embroidery, golf, dancing, ceramics, investing, gourmet cooking, cartooning, self-hypnotism, or any subject that any substantial number of people want to learn. And for all that how-to programming, going 24 hours a day, 365 days a year, people will be needed to write the scripts and to perform the practical demonstrations. That means *a lot* of how-to work! The rewards, in publicity and in cash, could be enormous.

## Editing

If your English is good, and you live in a city, you may be able to find some work as a freelance editor for a regional book publisher. Some of these firms have little or no permanent staff; they farm out most of the work to reliable part-timers.

By doing some part-time editorial work, you gain inside knowledge of the mechanics and finances of publishing; that knowledge will be an asset to you in your main line of work as a writer.

Moreover, the whole publishing business, national and regional, is a network of connections and acquaintances. There are people who worked together and still correspond ten or twenty years later; editors and publishers strike up acquaintance at book fairs, conventions, summer schools, etc. They exchange gossip, information, and predictions about the people, the trends, the economic and cultural conditions that determine the health or sickness of the publishing business. The average writer does not even realize that such inter-communication takes place. Yet through this process, writers' reputations are made and broken.

Now, what an advantage for the writer who can make even a loose connection with the business in the role of editor! Even if you are not already an experienced editor, *you can learn*. There are good books about the art and craft of editing. Get one or two and study them.

Then volunteer to work on some little magazine or bulletin published near you. Many community, charitable, religious, sport, hobby, and cultural organizations produce such magazines, and they are nearly all short on editorial assistance.

Don't demand the editor's chair right away! Offer to do anything, even if it's only stuffing envelopes and licking stamps. Listen; observe; ask questions. You will be getting information from people involved in the practical business of publishing.

With any luck you will soon be taking a hand in the real work of editing. Do it well; try to think like an editor. Save copies of the issues or sections that you edited. (And, of course, through this process you can let it be known that you are also able and willing to do some writing! Very soon you will find opportunities to get some of your work in print.)

Now, with this experience behind you, and samples of finished work in hand, you are ready to approach a commercial publisher. He will tell you in detail what he wants done, and will supervise your first efforts or will set another of his part-timers to supervise you.

Here, as in most branches of writing and publishing, you are not expected to be a genius! What's required is a modicum of technical knowledge, plus patience, perseverance, and the willingness to accept direction.

## Accounting

Good writing, plus sound marketing strategy, will infallibly earn money for you. That's exciting, sure enough! But you can't afford to forget that writing involves expenses.

Desks, typewriters, ribbons, recorders, sound tapes, paper, postage, phone calls, reference books, questionnaires, photocopying, and other research activities all cost money. Cameras, film, and photo processing cost money. Renting, lighting, and heating the work space cost money. (Even if you work in your own home, you are not getting *free* work space!)

And then, what about your time? Time is money!

Some writers drift along, always in a financial muddle, never knowing how much they are earning or spending. But that won't do for us. We are how-to writers; our specialty is to know precisely, and explain clearly, how things should be done.

### Keeping Accounts

Here are the basic elements of a simple system of accounts.

(a) A record of all income from your writing.

(b) A record of all expenditures for your writing.

(c) Supporting evidence for items (a) and (b). Keep receipts, invoices, cash register slips, transport-ticket duplicates, restaurant check stubs, telephone receipts, publishers' statements, etc. In short, whenever you receive or make a payment, try to get some kind of written evidence for it.

Keep all these pieces of evidence arranged systematically so that you can lay hands on any one of them when you need it.

You can obtain instruction on the technicalities of accounting from books or night school; or perhaps you can ask some friend to help you get started.

### Taxation

Details of tax legislation vary in different jurisdictions—from city to city, state to state, nation to nation. But here are some general hints:

(a) If you write at home and are for the moment earning nothing, your writing will probably be regarded as a hobby, and you will not have to bother about taxes.

(b) If you rent an office separate from your home, you may attract the attention of the authorities. You may find yourself billed for a business license or some such levy even if you are operating at a loss.

(c) As soon as you start showing a profit, you will probably be liable for income tax.

But *don't wait* for stage (c) to start keeping those accounts! You never know when you may have a sudden windfall—the unexpectedly big success of some book, a lucrative series of TV bookings, a well-paid series of lectures, etc.

Then, if you have good records from way back, you may be able to write off some of those past losses against your present income, and so save a lot of tax.

## Building a Reputation

From the time that you mail out your first script, you are starting to build a reputation with thousands of people you do not know, and will never meet. Let's look first at those who work in the publishing business. What qualities do they like to see in a writer?

## Reliability

I am deliberately putting reliability first. Over and over again, a writer of B-grade talent will beat out an A-grade competitor simply by *delivering the goods.*

It's no use being a highly trained genius if you cannot produce, and deliver to editors, *the right scripts, on time.*

As I use it here, the adjective "right" implies:

(a) On *the right subject.* Maybe that sounds obvious, yet many writers have not grasped it. The editor of a big how-to magazine visited a writers' conference looking for writers. (Mark that, please: an editor, *looking for writers!*) Scores of applicants came to her, bearing autobiographies, novels, history books, short stories, poems, etc.—maybe well-enough written in themselves, but *not what she needed.*

*Three* writers offered useful how-to ideas!

So you see, though the competition may be sizable, much of it is very weak. This editor told me, "Anyone with a well-prepared, businesslike presentation can get a hearing."

Here again, the word "businesslike" implies "dealing with the right kind of subject."

(b) In *the right style.* You discover the right style by studying the magazine you are aiming at. For a book publisher, you study the style range of the books he already has in print. Your final script maintains the style of your query (or whatever modification of it has been agreed upon).

(c) *The right length.* Deliver the length that the editor has approved. Shortages or excesses make more work for the editor, maybe more work for you; and they contribute to your reputation as being *unreliable.*

Now for delivery *on time.* Magazine and book editors work to elaborate schedules running months, or years, into the future. They love to see a script arriving just when it is needed! They do not enjoy being forced to chase and nag unreliable writers into producing overdue scripts. Each time *you* have to be chased and nagged, there's another smear on your reputation.

## Courtesy

Try to be courteous and cooperative in your dealings with editors. Realize that editors are not, as some writers suggest, two-headed, fork-tailed monsters who delight in humiliating and annoying writers.

Editors are, in fact, fairly ordinary human beings, trying to do a complex job in the face of many difficulties, technical and personal. Many editors are former writers; many are currently writing, in addition to their editorial duties. By my observation, editors understand the writer's problems far better than the average writer understands the editor's.

Courtesy and cooperation include the following:

(a) Prompt, accurate answers to letters from the editor.

(b) Recognition of the fact that the editor probably knows more than you do about editing books or magazines.

(c) Recognition of the fact that the editor cannot control *everybody* and *everything* concerned with the publication of your article or book. Mistakes may be made by printers and binders; there can be delays in distribution of finished books and magazines. The editor is not to blame if some reviewer pans your book; so don't bombard him with furious phone calls or letters.

Try to be courteous, too, in your dealings with *readers*. It is part of an author's business to send polite replies to people who write you about your book. Give thanks for compliments, answer questions, try to find tactful answers to criticisms. (Bear in mind that a reader's criticism may sometimes give you the idea for a revised, improved edition of the book.)

Magazine articles can produce correspondence, too, either as letters to the editor, or as letters to you, sent via the magazine. The same rules apply for these.

Bear in mind that, in all these transactions with editors and readers, you are creating your reputation. Your reputation is the average of other people's opinions of you.

A bad reputation hinders your career; a good reputation boosts it.

## Summary

Writing success takes time and money.
Learn to type fast and well.
Take lots of writing instruction.
Practice to attain writing fluency.
Diversify your selling.
Establish a writing production line.
You can launch your career without an agent.
Take time to learn public speaking.
Teaching is a form of research, and a mark of authority.
Radio and TV are potential how-to markets.
Freelance editing can be a profitable sideline.
Accurate accounts save tax trouble
Reliability and courtesy toward editors enhance your reputation.

# 16

# Progress Report

Here you can check your progress toward the goal. Fill in, on the appropriate line, the dates when you begin and finish the various exercises. I know that a few of them—for example, the operation of the publishing information file and the writing production line—have no finishing dates; you keep them going permanently. For such ongoing items, leave the right-hand column blank.

The personal report will stimulate you to carry the program through. Go to it—and good luck! Write me, in the care of Writer's Digest Books, about your success.

|  | Chapter 1 | Begun | Done |
|---|---|---|---|
| 1:1 | Study how-to authors | ___ | ___ |
| 1:2 | Personal qualifications | ___ | ___ |
|  | **Chapter 2** | Begun | Done |
| 2:1 | List of supplies | ___ | ___ |
|  | **Chapter 3** | Begun | Done |
| 3:1 | Newspaper & magazine reader profile | ___ | ___ |
| 3:2 | Published sample theme | ___ | ___ |
| 3:3 | Your theme | ___ | ___ |
| 3:4 | Published sample opening | ___ | ___ |
| 3:5 | Your opening | ___ | ___ |
| 3:6 | Sample body analysis | ___ | ___ |
| 3:7 | Your body plan | ___ | ___ |

| | | Begun | Done |
|---|---|---|---|
| 3:8 | Sample conclusion analysis | ___ | ___ |
| 3:9 | Your conclusion plan | ___ | ___ |
| 3:10 | Find potential markets | ___ | ___ |
| 3:11 | Article query letter | ___ | ___ |
| 3:12 | Draft & revise article | ___ | ___ |
| 3:13 | Follow editor's letter | ___ | ___ |
| 3:14 | Book review | ___ | ___ |

**Chapter 4**  Begun  Done

| | | Begun | Done |
|---|---|---|---|
| 4:1 | Analyze the competition | ___ | ___ |
| 4:2 | Analyze competitors' readership | ___ | ___ |
| 4:3 | Define your readership | ___ | ___ |
| 4:4 | Subject definition | ___ | ___ |
| 4:5 | Exemplary Dozen subject definition | ___ | ___ |
| 4:6 | Your book outline | ___ | ___ |
| 4:7 | Chapter subjects | ___ | ___ |
| 4:8 | Chapter summaries | ___ | ___ |
| 4:9 | Chapter titles | ___ | ___ |
| 4:10 | Chapter files | ___ | ___ |
| 4:11 | Competitors' wordage | ___ | ___ |
| 4:12 | Estimate total wordage | ___ | ___ |
| 4:13 | Estimate chapter wordage | ___ | ___ |

**Chapter 5**  Begun  Done

| | | Begun | Done |
|---|---|---|---|
| 5:1 | List suitable publishers | ___ | ___ |
| 5:2 | Proposal letter | ___ | ___ |
| 5:3 | Title page | ___ | ___ |
| 5:4 | Outline for proposal | ___ | ___ |
| 5:5 | Synopsis for proposal | ___ | ___ |
| 5:6 | Sample section | ___ | ___ |

**Chapter 6**  Begun  Done

| | | Begun | Done |
|---|---|---|---|
| 6:1 | Publishing information file | ___ | ___ |
| 6:2 | Exemplary Dozen: publishing history | ___ | ___ |
| 6:3 | Study how-to advertising | ___ | ___ |
| 6:4 | Exemplary Dozen: publicity study | ___ | ___ |

**Chapter 8**  Begun  Done

| | | Begun | Done |
|---|---|---|---|
| 8:1 | Collaborator assessment | ___ | ___ |
| 8:2 | Ghostwriting time | ___ | ___ |
| 8:3 | Ghostwriting fee | ___ | ___ |

**Chapter 9**  Begun  Done

| | | Begun | Done |
|---|---|---|---|
| 9:1 | Study l-r how-to books and publishers | ___ | ___ |
| 9:2 | Start files on l-r how-to subjects | ___ | ___ |
| 9:3 | Plan direct-approach interview | ___ | ___ |

| | Chapter 10 | Begun | Done |
|---|---|---|---|
| 10:1 | Notes on materials, etc. | —— | —— |
| 10:2 | Notes on working conditions | —— | —— |
| 10:3 | Notes on working methods | —— | —— |
| 10:4 | Notes on working difficulties | —— | —— |
| 10:5 | Page of rough draft | —— | —— |
| 10:6 | Page-numbering system | —— | —— |
| 10:7 | Wordage-control system | —— | —— |
| 10:8 | Rewrite a chapter | —— | —— |
| 10:9 | Begin index | —— | —— |
| 10:10 | Regular notebook use | —— | —— |
| 10:11 | Getting started | —— | —— |

| | Chapter 11 | Begun | Done |
|---|---|---|---|
| 11:1 | Clipping file | —— | —— |
| 11:2 | Reference book list | —— | —— |
| 11:3 | Library exploration | —— | —— |
| 11:4 | Misc. writing records file | —— | —— |
| 11:5 | Questionnaire draft | —— | —— |
| 11:6 | Preparation for interview | —— | —— |
| 11:7 | Questions for interview | —— | —— |
| 11:8 | Practice interview | —— | —— |
| 11:9 | Exemplary Dozen copyright study | —— | —— |

| | Chapter 12 | Begun | Done |
|---|---|---|---|
| 12:1 | Modern style rewrite | —— | —— |
| 12:2 | Exemplary Dozen sentence length | —— | —— |
| 12:3 | Your sentence length | —— | —— |
| 12:4 | Exemplary Dozen paragraph length | —— | —— |
| 12:5 | Your paragraph length | —— | —— |
| 12:6 | Sentence analysis | —— | —— |
| 12:7 | Punctuation marks | —— | —— |
| 12:8 | Titles, etc. | —— | —— |
| 12:9 | Check spelling | —— | —— |
| 12:10 | Concise style | —— | —— |
| 12:11 | Specific terms | —— | —— |
| 12:12 | Check consistency | —— | —— |
| 12:13 | Tape-recording test | —— | —— |
| 12:14 | Ben Franklin exercise | —— | —— |

| | Chapter 13 | Begun | Done |
|---|---|---|---|
| 13:1 | Exemplary Dozen illustration study | —— | —— |

| | Chapter 14 | Begun | Done |
|---|---|---|---|
| 14:1 | Study Exemplary Dozen promotion | —— | —— |
| 14:2 | Plan your promotional material | —— | —— |

| | | Begun | Done |
|---|---|---|---|
| 14:3 | Draft promotional leaflet | ___ | ___ |
| 14:4 | Practice broadcast interview | ___ | ___ |
| | **Chapter 15** | Begun | Done |
| 15:1 | Fluency drill | ___ | ___ |
| 15:2 | Writing production line | ___ | ___ |

# Recommended Reading

**Publishers and Publishing**

*Bookmaking: The Illustrated Guide to Design and Production*, by Marshall Lee. (Bowker, 1979)

*How to Get Happily Published*, by Judith Appelbaum & Nancy Evans. (Harper & Row, 1978)

*A Practical Style Guide for Authors and Editors*, by Margaret Nicholson. (Holt, 1967)

*The Publish-It-Yourself Handbook*, edited by Bill Henderson. (Pushcart Press, 1973)

*What Happens in Book Publishing*, edited by Chandler B. Grannis. (Columbia University Press, 1967)

*A Writer's Guide to Book Publishing*, by Richard Balkin. (Hawthorn, 1977)

**Article Writing**

*Book Reviewing*, edited by Sylvia E. Kamerman. (The Writer, 1978)

*A Complete Guide to Marketing Magazine Articles*, by Duane Newcomb. (Writer's Digest, 1975)

*How to Write and Sell for the Out-of-Doors*, by Jack Denton Scott. (Macmillan, 1962)

*Magazine Article Writing*, by Betsy P. Graham. (Holt, Rinehart, 1980)

*Magazine Writing Today*, by Jerome E. Kelley. (Writer's Digest, 1978)

*Sell Copy*, by Webster Kuswa. (Writer's Digest, 1979)
*Write On Target*, by Connie Emerson. (Writer's Digest, 1981)
*Writing and Selling Non-Fiction*, by Hayes B. Jacobs. (Writer's Digest, 1975)
*Writing Articles That Sell*, by Louise Boggess. (Prentice-Hall, 1965)

## Marketing Information

*The Canadian Writer's Guide.* (Fitzhenry & Whiteside, 1979)
*Literary Market Place.* (Bowker, annual)
*Writer's Market.* (Writer's Digest, annual)
*Writer's Yearbook.* (Writer's Digest, annual)

## Working Methods

"How I Write" (essay) in *Portraits from Memory*, by Bertrand Russell. (Allen & Unwin, 1958)
*Human Potentialities*, by Gardner Murphy. (Basic Books, 1958)
"The Philosophy of Composition" (essay), by Edgar Allan Poe, in *Edgar Allan Poe, Selected & Edited*, by Philip Van Doren Stern. (Penguin, 1977)

## Research & General Reference

*The Canada Year Book.* (Information Canada, annual)
*The Craft of Interviewing*, by John Brady. (Writer's Digest, 1975)
*Law and the Writer*, edited by Kirk Polking and Leonard S. Meranus. (Writer's Digest, 1981)
*Plagiarism and Originality*, by Alexander Lindey. (Harper, 1952)
*The People's Almanac*, by David Wallechinsky & Irving Wallace. (Bantam, 1978)
*The World Almanac & Book of Facts.* (Newspaper Enterprise Association, annual)

## Style

*The Art of Plain Talk*, by Rudolf Flesch. (Macmillan, 1962)
*The Art of Readable Writing*, by Rudolf Flesch. (Macmillan, 1962)
*Bartlett's Familiar Quotations*, by John Bartlett. (Little, Brown, 1968)
*A Dictionary of Modern English Usage*, by H.W. Fowler. (Oxford University Press, 1965)
*The Elements of Style*, by W. Strunk Jr. & E.B. White. (Macmillan, 1978)
*How to Be Brief*, by Rudolf Flesch. (Harper, 1962)

*How to Write for the World of Work,* by Thomas E. Pearsall & Donald H. Cunningham. (Holt, Rinehart, 1978)

*Roget's Thesaurus of English Words & Phrases.* (St. Martin, 1977)

*Successful Technical Writing,* by Tyler G. Hicks. (McGraw-Hill, 1959)

*A Way with Words,* by Bill Cameron. (Western Producer Prairie Books, 1979)

*Word Power Made Easy,* by Norman Lewis. (Doubleday, 1978)

*Writing for Results,* by David W. Ewing. (John Wiley & Sons, 1974)

## Illustrations

*Basic Black and White Photography,* by Karl M. Rehm. (American Photographic Book Publishing Co., 1976)

*How You Can Make $25,000 a Year With Your Camera No Matter Where You Live,* by Larry Cribb. (Writer's Digest, 1981)

*Learning Photography,* by Antoine Desilets. (Habitex Books, 1977)

*Photocommunications,* by David H. Carl. (Macmillan, 1979)

*The Photographer's Handbook,* by John Hedgecoe. (Knopf, 1977)

*Photographer's Market.* (Writer's Digest, annual)

*The Writer-Photographer,* by John Milton. (Chilton, 1972)

# Other Writer's Digest Books

**Market Directories**
Artist's Market, 528 pp. $13.95
Fiction Writer's Market, 504 pp. $15.95
Photographer's Market, 576 pp. $14.95
Songwriter's Market, 432 pp. $12.95
Writer's Market, 936 pp. $17.95

**General Writing Books**
Beginning Writer's Answer Book, 264 pp. $9.95
How to Get Started in Writing, 180 pp. $10.95
Law and the Writer, 240 pp. (paper) $7.95
Make Every Word Count, 256 pp. (paper) $6.95
Treasury of Tips for Writers, (paper), 174 pp. $6.95
Writer's Resource Guide, 488 pp. $12.95

**Magazine/News Writing**
Complete Guide to Marketing Magazine Articles, 248 pp. $9.95
Craft of Interviewing, 244 pp. $9.95
Magazine Writing: The Inside Angle, 256 pp. $10.95
Magazine Writing Today, 220 pp. $9.95
Newsthinking: The Secret of Great Newswriting, 204 pp. $11.95
1001 Article Ideas, 270 pp. $10.95
Stalking the Feature Story, 310 pp. $9.95
Write on Target, 240 pp. $12.95
Writing and Selling Non-Fiction, 317 pp. $10.95

**Fiction Writing**
Creating Short Fiction, 228 pp. $11.95
Handbook of Short Story Writing, (paper), 238 pp. $6.95
How to Write Best-Selling Fiction, 300 pp. $13.95
How to Write Short Stories that Sell, 212 pp. $9.95
One Way to Write Your Novel, 138 pp. (paper) $6.95
Secrets of Successful Fiction, 119 pp. $8.95
Writing the Novel: From Plot to Print, 197 pp. $10.95

## Category Writing Books

**Cartoonist's and Gag Writer's Handbook**, (paper), 157 pp. $9.95
**Children's Picture Book: How to Write It, How to Sell It**, 224 pp. $16.95
**Confession Writer's Handbook**, 173 pp. $9.95
**Guide to Greeting Card Writing**, 256 pp. $10.95
**Guide to Writing History**, 258 pp. $9.95
**How to Write and Sell Your Personal Experiences**, 226 pp. $10.95
**How to Write "How-To" Books and Articles**, 192 pp. (paper) $8.95
**Mystery Writer's Handbook**, 273 pp. $9.95
**The Poet and the Poem**, 399 pp. $11.95
**Poet's Handbook**, 224 pp. $10.95
**Sell Copy**, 205 pp. $11.95
**Successful Outdoor Writing**, 244 pp. $11.95
**Travel Writer's Handbook**, 274 pp. $11.95
**TV Scriptwriter's Handbook**, 322 pp. $11.95
**Writing and Selling Science Fiction**, 191 pp. $8.95
**Writing for Children & Teenagers**, 269 pp. $9.95

## The Writing Business

**Complete Handbook for Freelance Writers**, 391 pp. $14.95
**How to Be a Successful Housewife/Writer**, 254 pp. $10.95
**How You Can Make $20,000 a Year Writing (No Matter Where You Live)**, 270 pp. (paper) $6.95
**Jobs For Writers**, 281 pp. $11.95
**Profitable Part-time/Full-time Freelancing**, 195 pp. $10.95
**Writer's Digest Diary**, 144 pp. $14.95

## Photography Books

**How You Can Make $25,000 a Year with Your Camera (No Matter Where You Live)**, 224 pp. (paper) $9.95
**Sell & Re-Sell Your Photos**, 323 pp. $14.95

To order directly from the publisher, include $1.25 postage and handling for 1 book and 50¢ for each additional book. Allow 30 days for delivery.

For a current catalog of books for writers or information on *Writer's Digest* magazine, *Writer's Yearbook*, Writer's Digest School correspondence courses or manuscript criticism, write to:

**Writer's Digest Books, Department B**
**9933 Alliance Road, Cincinnati OH 45242**

Prices subject to change without notice.

# Index